GOD REALLY LOVES US

by
William Browning, C.P.

THE LITURGICAL PRESS
Collegeville, Minnesota

DEDICATION

To St. Paul of the Cross, Father and Founder of the Passionists, to all my Passionist brethren with whom I share life, and to those many others who, by accepting and loving me, have helped me to grow from knowledge to conviction that GOD REALLY LOVES US.

The material in this book originally appeared in SISTERS TODAY, published with ecclesiastical approval by the monks of St. John's Abbey, Collegeville, Minnesota.

Copyright © 1979, The Order of St. Benedict, Inc., Collegeville, Minnesota.

ISBN: 0-8146-1049-8

Scriptural quotations are from the New American Bible, copyright © Confraternity of Christian Doctrine, 1970.
Printed by Sentinel Printing Company, St. Cloud, Minnesota.

TABLE OF CONTENTS

INTRODUCTION

In the book of Sirach we read: "Before you die, be good to your friend and give him a share in what you possess" (Sir. 14:13). No words could better express my feeling on seeing this small collection of my writings published.

Each of the chapters of this book was written as an article at various intervals over a period of some six years. Each chapter expresses an insight of the moment that was very significant in my own spiritual journey. In some instances the insight came as a ray of light when all seemed dark. In a very true sense I consider these writings autobiographical.

As the articles appeared individually I became aware that the insights given me also helped others. That they now appear together in this book is due entirely to the encouragement of many who urged that they be printed in book form.

The title for this book was selected, not by myself, but by the publishers. Their choice gives me particular satisfaction because I feel that the title expresses the deepest conviction to which my own search has led me.

It is with sincere gratitude that I share with a wider audience these insights that have meant so much to me along the way.

William Browning, C.P.

God

Really Loves Us

Deep in the heart of most of us there is a lurking feeling that all the things we hear and say about God's love for us are not really true. Who of us has not many times tried to reassure others in their depression that God really loves them? We easily nod assent when we hear the statement that God loves us, that is, if we keep it general enough and do not think of it in terms of ourselves. It is when we try to assent to the statements, "God loves *me*" that our lurking feeling begins to assert itself. Deep down, many of us are not really that sure.

Father Van Breemen in his book *As Bread That Is Broken* very perceptively says, "It is not enough to have but just once touched the love of God. There is more required to build one's life on God's love. It takes a long time to believe that I am accepted by God as I am" (p. 13.)

Reasons For Our Reluctance

When we search for the reasons why we are so reluctant to accept the personal love of God for us, they can be found at many possible sources. Most of them are deeply rooted in our own personal experience. In one way or another, they all have to do with our thoughts and feelings about God and about ourselves.

We are increasingly aware of the hazardous course through which our education and formation have led us. Some of us may have had an early childhood experience that is largely responsible. It could be something so ordinary as negative attitudes toward God developed when we were children. An example would be an experience in which someone used fear of God and his punishments as a motive to get us to behave ourselves. Such experiences can leave a lifelong impression that can be very difficult to slough off.

Maybe even more commonly we can find the source of such distrust in our own experience of ourselves. All of us have a history, and that history has shaped our attitudes. Our histories may differ greatly from one person to another, but we all have in common the unfolding experience of sin.

As we have had to face the reality of sin, it has not left us unaffected. Even though many of us may have been led through sin to some awareness of redemption, in most of us sin has left a deadly residue of self-depreciation. We so very easily transfer our distrust of ourselves to God. As a result, personal assent to that simple statement, "God loves me," can be an extremely difficult step to make.

So much depends on whether we make this personal assent or not. It makes the difference between a life that is lived in fear and paralysis of spirit or one that is lived in the fresh air of the freedom of God's children.

The Reaction Of Fear, Not Guilt

It is interesting to note that in the earliest account of human sin related in the Scriptures, the reaction to it was not so much one of guilt as of fear. Just after the account of the disobedience of our first parents, we read this passage in the book of Genesis: "When they heard the sound of the Lord God moving about in the garden at the breezy time of the day, the man and his wife hid themselves from the Lord God among the trees of the garden. The Lord God called to the man and asked him, 'Where are you?' He answered, 'I heard you in the garden, but I was afraid, because I was naked, so I hid myself'" (Gen. 3:8-10). Symbolically this expresses the reaction of every person to the experience of sin. The sinner, and that is all of us, feels naked, is afraid and tries to hide from God.

This reaction of fear in face of sin is not present only in the beginning. It continues to recur throughout the Scriptures. It was fear that led the people to build the Tower of Babel (Gen. 11). They felt that if they could build a tower high enough they would be on a level with God and would no longer have to fear him. The idolatry that seemed never to be far from the people of Israel was motivated by fear. They feared that they could not really trust God and they wanted to cultivate all possible friends just in case.

In spite of the fact that redemption has been so marvellously manifested in Christ, we today can still act in much the same way as God's people of old. In this respect, we are not far removed from our Old Testament forebears.

The Central Message Of Scripture

The pattern of Scriptural revelation seems to have been very much shaped by this ever present fear with which God had to deal with his people. The result is that the overwhelming message of the Scriptures, both Old and New Testaments, is that God really loves his people. He keeps saying over and over again that he really loves them and that this love reaches out to them, not as they might be if they were better, but that he loves them as they are and where they are.

The love God reveals is not one that is deserved or merited but is a free gift that is in no way conditioned by anything in his people. That beautiful message in Deuteronomy comes to mind in which God gives the only explanation he ever offers of the reason for his love: "You are a people sacred to the Lord your God; for he has chosen you from all the nations on the face of the earth to be a people peculiarly his own. It was not because you are the largest of all nations that the Lord set his heart on you and chose you, for you are really the smallest of all nations. It was because the Lord loved you . . ." (Dt. 7:6-8). In other words, he is saying, "It is nothing in you, it is my free gift."

Old Testament Examples

The Old Testament revelation revolves around the three great themes of Creation, Exodus, and Covenant. Each of these themes is a manifestation of God's love for his people in action.

By creation God communicates his own life to his people. He does this not just in the act of making from nothing in the beginning, but he continues his creative work in all that he does for the building up of his people.

The Exodus expresses his love in the form of deliverance from slavery. In Egypt the slavery is physical, but the Scriptures keep pointing to the Exodus as a sign of the greater spiritual deliverance that will come in the person of the Messiah.

The Covenant is God's love in action in the form of a pledge of fidelity never to abandon his people: "I will be your God and you shall be my people." This fidelity is absolute, proven a thousand times over, even in face of the repeated infidelity of the people. This fidelity is grasped so beautifully in the Wisdom of Sirach: "Study the generations long past and understand; has anyone hoped in the Lord and been disappointed? Has anyone persevered in his fear and been forsaken? Has anyone called upon him and been rebuffed? Compassionate and merciful is the Lord; he forgives sins, he saves in time of trouble" (Sir. 2:10-11).

Some Striking Texts

What God does in action in his great works of Creation, Exodus and Covenant, he also expresses time and again in word, and that in the most endearing terms. Such words are everywhere in the Old Testament. Let us here reflect upon only a few striking texts.

When the chosen people reached Sinai, God said to Moses, "Thus shall you say to the house of Jacob; tell the Israelites: You have seen for yourselves how I treated the Egyptians and how I bore you up on eagle wings and brought you here to myself. Therefore, if you hearken to my voice and keep my covenant, you shall be my special possession, dearer to me than all other people, though all the earth is mine. You shall be to me a kingdom of priests, a holy nation" (Ex. 19:3-6).

Since one of the great missions of the prophets is to call the people to fidelity, they speak repeatedly of God's love as a motive for this. Texts abound, and we must content ourselves here with citing just a few examples. Isaiah speaks these words of God: "Though the mountains leave their place and the hills be shaken, my love shall never leave you nor my covenant of peace be shaken, says the Lord, who has mercy on you" (Is. 54:10).

Also in Isaiah God uses the most emotion-laden image possible to protest his love: "Can a mother forget her infant so as to be without tenderness for the child of her womb? Even should she forget, I will never forget you. See, upon the palms of my hands I have written your name; your walls are ever before me" (Is. 49:15-16).

Psalm 103 gives us a moving expression of God's love for his people, and it focuses specifically upon the unmerited aspect of that love. In other words, it centers on the love of God when confronted with human sinfulness. "Merciful and gracious is the Lord, slow to anger and abounding in kindness. He will not always chide, nor does he keep his wrath forever. Not according to our sins does he deal with us, nor does he requite us according to our crimes. For as the heavens are high above the earth, so surpassing is his kindness toward those who fear him. As far as the east is from the west, so far has he put our transgressions from us. As a father has compassion on his children, so the Lord has compassion on those who fear him, for he knows how we are formed; he remembers that we are dust" (Ps. 103:8-14).

"Fear Not, I Will Be With You."

Before leaving our reflection on the Old Testament message of God's love, a word should be said about an expression that is repeated there time and again and is continued into the New Testament. The statement is: "Fear not, I will be with you." God's people seemed always to be afraid, and God never tired of saying to them, "Do not be afraid." He says this to Abraham, Moses, Isaiah, Jeremiah and many others.

Let us consider only this beautiful text from Isaiah: "But you, Israel, my servant, Jacob whom

I have chosen, offspring of Abraham my friend —
you whom I have taken from the ends of the
earth and summoned from its far-off places, you
whom I have called my servant, whom I have
chosen and will not cast off — Fear not, I am
with you; be not dismayed; I am your God. I will
strengthen you, and help you, and uphold you
with my right hand of justice . . . . For I am the
Lord, your God, who grasp your right hand; it is I
who say to you, 'Fear not, I will help you'" (Is.
41:8-10, 13).

What is so striking about this and many other
similar texts is not so much what is said as the
cadenced intensity with which it is said. It is almost as if God is saying, "I know it is hard for
you to believe this, but it is really true. I do love
you, and I will take care of you."

After reflecting on these texts from the Old
Testament, it should be easy to see how the
statement, sometimes so glibly made, that the Old
Testament is a time of justice, while the New
Testament is one of mercy, can hardly be sus-
tained. The God of the Old Testament never tires
of protesting his love for his people.

The New Testament Message

When we turn to the New Testament, we find
the ultimate effort on the part of God to convey
to his people the reality and the depth of his
love. In a real sense all that he had done and
said to his people of old had not really gotten
through to them. But then God sent his own Son
into the world.

Many interpretations could be put on the meaning of the incarnation. One very true one would be to say that God sent his Son so that his message of love would no longer be a matter of words. It would take on, in the person of Jesus, the visible, tangible form of evidence that humans crave and that could not be denied.

For thirty years Jesus lived among his people. He had the face, the hands and the heart of a human being with which to give expression to the love of his Father. People could not only hear what he said and see what he did. They could look into his face and see there the human manifestation of the merciful love of God.

The works that Jesus did had as their purpose to show that his Father's love was real. No one was too small or insignificant or sinful to escape his loving care and concern. As he healed the sick, raised the dead and forgave the sinner, he was saying in action, "My Father is your Father and he loves you." When he spoke, it was evident to those who heard him that this Jesus was not like any ordinary man. Somehow, his very presence spoke of the God of whom his humanity was in the fullest sense a sacrament or sign.

The Parables Of Jesus

It was especially in his great parables that Jesus brought home so forcefully the truth and the depth of God's love. He used the simplest human images and experiences to give flesh to that love. He chose, for example, to use the image of a shepherd, so familiar to his hearers, to bring home the Father's love. They knew the devotion of a shepherd to his sheep. Jesus dared to say, "I am the good shepherd. I know my sheep and my sheep know me . . . for these sheep I will give my life" (Jn. 10:14-15).

In another place he makes this image all the more explicit: "Who among you, if he has a hundred sheep and loses one of them, does not leave the ninety-nine in the wasteland and follow the lost one until he finds it? And when he finds it, he puts in on his shoulders in jubilation. Once arrived home, he invites friends and neighbors in and says to them, 'Rejoice with me because I have found my sheep.'" And lest the very simplicity of the image might lead them to delight only in the story, he makes the explicit application: "I tell you, there will likewise be more joy in heaven over one repentant sinner than over ninety-nine righteous people who have no need to repent" (Lk. 15:4-7). Those who heard these words must have remembered them many times, especially when they looked out and saw a shepherd leading his flock.

The Prodigal Son

Perhaps in no parable did Jesus speak of the Father's love so vividly as in the parable of the Prodigal Son. And it is a parable that relates to the experience of every man and woman. We all know this parable almost by heart, but we need to read and ponder it time and time again. Almost every time we read and pray over it, we will see something new in it.

The parable touches all the elements of the human experience of sin: the impetuosity and shortsightedness with which the son requested his share of the inheritance; the haste with which he squandered everything with no thought of the consequences; the sudden awareness of what he had done; the feeling of unworthiness that prevented his even considering that his father might still love him.

When the son decides to go back home from the sheer motive of survival, he very carefully prepares a speech. That speech never even considers the possibility of anything but rejection by his father.

The real grandeur of the parable is revealed when he actually does return. Jesus is very explicit in saying that "When the son was still a long way off, the father saw him." In other words, the father was waiting all along for his son's return; he never ceased to love this wayward son and hope for his return. He goes out to meet his son and embraces him. When the son tries to make his carefully prepared speech, he is interrupted. His father is not interested in it. A celebration is called for the simple reason that "This son of mine was dead and has come back to life. He was lost and is found" (Cf. Lk. 15:11-30).

This is the parable of every man and woman. If seriously pondered over and over again, it leaves no room for continued doubt about the real attitude of God our Father toward us.

The Drama Of Love

Jesus' life among us has been an unfolding drama of love. Saint John, when he introduces the Passover meal from which came the Eucharist, is careful to tell us, "He had loved his own in this world, and would show his love for them to the end" (Jn. 13:1). He showed that love by giving them, and the Church after them, the memorial of his immolation unto death. Then he walked resolutely to his own death as the supreme expression of his love for which he had come. Every crucifix stands as an undeniable reminder that the Father's love for us is real.

The lesson of all that we have been here considering is summed up in the following words of Pope Paul VI: "The Good News is this: that God loves us; that he became man to share in our life and to share our life with us; that therefore we are not alone, for God is present in our entire history — that of peoples and that of individuals; and that he will bring us, if we allow him, to an eternal happiness beyond human expectation."

God Loves Me Now!

Before concluding our reflections, it may be well to repeat a point alluded to before and state it more emphatically. For unless we grasp this point, the lesson will remain in the realm of mere theory and will not affect our lives at all. The point is this: God really and truly loves me. But he loves me, not as I dream of being, or as I might be if I had led a better life, but as I am here and now with all my weaknesses and sins.

It is this conviction, deeply internalized, and it alone, that can dispel the clouds of darkness and gloom that so often surround us and make us doubt ourselves and God. Only this can lead us out into the clear light of knowing that we are really loved by God. God gives us all the evidence of his love, but it does not become Good News to us until it finds roots deep within our hearts.

Let us end by returning to the Old Testament and pondering this beautiful text from Isaiah: "But now, thus says the Lord, who created you, O Jacob, and formed you, O Israel: Fear not, for I have redeemed you; I have called you by name: you are mine. When you pass through the water, I will be with you; in the rivers you shall not drown. When you walk through fire, you shall not be burned; the flames shall not consume you. For I am the Lord, your God, the Holy One of Israel, your savior" (Is. 43:1-3).

The greatest challenge of our life is this: will we accept the free gift of God's boundless love and come to know the peace and joy that this acceptance brings? Or will we cling to our doubts about this love and live joyless and gloomy lives? Our decision is literally a matter of life or death.

2

Meeting God
In The Inner Self

As we strive for a personal relationship with God, the simplest reflection tells us that two persons are involved: God and myself. We know, at least by faith, that God is absolute, faithful, unchanging, and that he could not but reach out eagerly to receive us as we come to him. We have difficulty in perceiving these realities about God, but at least our faith tells us that they are true and real. That is simply the way he has revealed himself to us.

On the other side of this exchange there is my own person, my *self*. From this side we are dealing with something quite different. By contrast to God, we find ourselves to be relative, unfaithful, changing, and sometimes far from inclined to accept God's embrace. This self is the center and the source of all the struggle and conflict that mark our spiritual journey.

Trying To Conquer God

We know theoretically that coming close to God is a matter of his moving toward us and taking possession of us rather than of our grasping him. But all too often, on the perception level, we think and act as if we have to conquer God. As a result, it takes a lot of being and living to grow in our personal relationship with God. The work of the spiritual masters has not been concerned so much with a problem of God as with the problems humans face when they approach God. To invoke a classical image, the real difficulty is in getting the wood disposed and accustomed to the fire that invades it.

My purpose here is not to single out and analyze the various problems we face in our spiritual journey. So much has been written about these already. Rather, I would like to discuss a matter that underlies all of our journey. It amounts to an attempt to share an insight that has become invaluable to myself in the hope that it might be equally helpful to others.

The central thought that I propose for reflection is this: maybe we have an altogether too limited notion of our *self*, of this person that is trying to reach out to God. And maybe, if we can broaden and deepen our awareness of our *self*, we can engage more peacefully and successfully in our journey to God.

The Meaning Of Self

When we think or speak of my *self*, we are referring to this person, this body-spirit, what we experience all the time. Although we do not usually analyze it very carefully, we tend to think of this self as a jumble of many elements, some of them very negative. Witness how often we try to deny words of praise spoken of us; or the ease with which most of us develop a negative self-image. These are symptoms of the way we tend to perceive ourselves in a negative way.

I would like to term what we are speaking of here our outer, surface self. I will even call it our superficial self for reasons that may be made clear later. It is the self in which all our struggles and conflicts are experienced, where our defeats are felt, with all the consequent frustration that follows on this. The self that we perceive in our daily experience is often anything but attractive.

The real danger is that we think of this outer self as the subject of our search for God. God can never be met only on that level. The problems we face there can never be solved by paying attention only to this outer layer of our being. These struggles are, for the most part, manifestations of subconscious emotional conflicts that are beyond our immediate understanding or control. I often remember a quote I read somewhere from Erich Fromm: "Most of what people have in their conscious minds is fiction and delusion . . . therefore consciousness as such has no particular value." This says volumes about what we are discussing.

Our True Self

We need to realize that our true self is much deeper than what we experience directly. We need to be aware of, come in contact with, this deep inner person that is the real me before God. This is the true self that alone can ever meet God and be one with him.

This inner self has been variously called by spiritual masters through the ages. They use terms like: depth or summit of the soul, the ground of our being, the center, the inner room of the castle. Mysterious as such a notion may seem at first, we must strive to grasp it if we wish to enter into a true relationship with God.

It is in this inner self that God dwells, that we experience full redemption, that the transforming grace of baptism has touched us. It is there that the beauty of God himself is reflected as in a mirror, or a pure ray of light. It is only there that we can truly meet God in deep communion. From this deep inner source our gifted goodness needs to work itself out to the surface and calm its conflicts. Any other approach limits us to fighting skirmishes that will never cease to recur.

Saint Paul the Apostle seems to have had an intuitive sense of what we are saying here. He expresses this in his beautiful prayer for the Ephesians:

That is why I kneel before the Father from whom every family in heaven and on earth takes its name; and I pray that he will bestow on you gifts in keeping with the riches of his glory. May he strengthen you *inwardly* through the working of his Spirit. May Christ dwell in your hearts through faith, and may charity be the root and foundation of your life. Thus you will be able to grasp fully, with all the holy ones, the breadth and length and height and depth of Christ's love, and experience this love which surpasses all knowledge, so that you may attain to the fullness of God himself (Eph. 3:14-19).

Paul seemed convinced that ideals such as he was praying for could not be experienced on the surface, but only in the *inner self*.

Thomas Merton stressed many times that we discover God only in our inner, true self. As an example of his thought: "Unless we discover this deep self, which is hidden with Christ in God, we will never really know ourselves as persons. Nor will we know God. For it is by the door of this deep self that we enter into the spiritual knowledge of God. (And indeed, if we seek our true selves it is not in order to contemplate ourselves, but to pass beyond ourselves and find Him)" (*The New Man*, p. 32).

We need, therefore, in our search for God, to be in touch with our true self and avoid the danger of becoming bogged down in preoccupation with the experienced self which is only on the surface.

The History Of Self

All of us are, in both our inner and outer self, the fruit and the summation of not only who we are but also of where we have been. On both levels we have had a history that has gradually and imperceptibly shaped us into what we are. It is important to realize that it is this person that we have become that must be related to God, not an ideal, theoretical one. In pursuit of a deeper understanding of the self, let us trace some of its history. Every personal history is different and it is this that makes each of us unique. But there is also enough communality in the human experience to allow us to trace such a history.

First of all, let us look at our deep inner self. At this deep inner point of our being each of us is a unique creation of the hands of God. As happened in the original work of creation, when God made each of us, "he looked upon us and saw that we were good." For most of us, in a matter of days or weeks we were introduced into the family of God through the saving waters of baptism. By this gift we were flooded with God's light and grace, we became children of God, and the unique grace of redemption was given us through the blood of Christ. God made us his dwelling place, more beautiful in his eyes than any earthly temple could ever be. Thus, in our origins all was brilliant, clear, bright and beautiful.

Grace Added To Grace

As time moved on in the personal history of this unique creation of God, our development was very much a matter of grace added to grace. Time came when the Bread of Life became our daily bread with all that this brought in the way of growth and development. We learned the beginner's lessons of communion with God in prayer.

As we moved on through life all of these elements of grace became interwoven with the very fabric of our life. Along with grace there was that manifold experience of goodness that came from the human family and the world into which we had been born—acceptance, love, friendship, and the goodness and the beauty of God's creation that fed our inner being through those wonderful gifts of God, the senses.

Of course, as all this was happening there were negative forces at play also. We were experiencing the effects of fallen nature through frailty and sin. But in hindsight we might rightly wonder if the harm this was doing us was more in the guilt we incurred than in the evil committed. It is important that we do not let the reality of sin blind us to all the good that we received. Furthermore, we must realize that the effects of sin are felt far more in our outer self than in that deep inner center that is God's dwelling place.

As our inner self was being formed, things were happening in the outer self as well. Its development was intricately tied up with our psychological and emotional history, and it is this which makes the outer self so very complicated. On this level, too, all the good we have mentioned was being experienced. But as fallen human beings we likely tended to focus more on the negative experiences than on the good. Even in infancy, and more so in childhood, we experienced some hurts, lack of acceptance, a sense of failure, and such things easily seared their mark in our subconscious.

In trying to cope with such experiences we tended to nurse our wounds, to form masks that would hide our feelings from others, and to play games with ourselves and others. So in a real sense, we were becoming two *selves*, the one of deep inner goodness and the other, which tended to dominate our consciousness, a superficial false self.

The Growth Of Self

We have focused mainly on infancy and childhood, and that is where the course is established. But as our life has gone on, this dual history has continued. As we grew into adulthood and its responsibilities, the gifts begun at our personal creation continued to come to us, further enriching the inner goodness that was ours from the beginning. Whether in marriage or in celibacy there was the enriching experience of love and friendship, as well as that of faithful service of others out of love.

With the broadening of education and experience, the goodness of the inner self remained and was further enriched. To the degree that we were open to receive and respond to beauty and goodness in all its forms, our own goodness and beauty were enhanced. But all of this was happening in a hidden way, as are all things in the inner self, and much of it escaped our direct notice or attention. Nonetheless, it was there and was following the law of all God's creative work: he made it, it was good, and he made it without repentance.

But as this growth and development of the inner self was taking place, the outer self continued in its own path of unfolding experience. At least intermittently, hurts continued to befall us, we were disappointed in ourselves for our failure to live up to our own dreams. Very likely the masks that we had formed earlier continued to harden, and the games we learned to play became more intricate and confusing even to ourselves. Because this outer self was so conspicuous and experienced so immediately, we easily began to think of it as our real self. And life seemed to become increasingly more complicated.

Our Concern For God

Along the way, as we began to develop an earnestness about the spiritual dimension of life, we became concerned about the place of God in our life. As our insight deepened, we became increasingly earnest in our desire for a personal relationship with God. We then entered on a spiritual journey that was an effort to relate this person that I call my *self* to God.

I think it is true to say that our degree of success in this venture has been determined by which self prevailed in our consciousness. Was it the deep inner self where all is ready and disposed for relationship with God, or the outer self where all the storms brew and the battles are waged? It may be well to recall at this point Merton's statement quoted previously that it is only in the inner true self that we will ever be able to know God.

Prayer And The Inner Self

These reflections have traced only the broad outlines of the genesis of the self, inner and outer. Hopefully the matter is sufficiently clear to move on to what is the main purpose of these reflections. Our main concern here is with the concept of the self as it affects our relationship with God.

The whole direction and success of our spiritual journey is worked out in our life of prayer. It is here that we truly meet God, values are embraced, and the light for decision is received. Most of all, it is here that we come to a stance of worship and love before the God who is the source of our life and the guide of our destiny.

None of this can be accomplished if we think only in terms of the outer self. On that level we are simply too fickle, there is too much falsehood at play. Besides, it is not there that God dwells as in his temple but in the inner depths of our being, in our deep inner self. This is not to say that regulation of the outer self is not important. But the taming of the exterior can only take place when it begins at the core of our being. Treatises that would leave the impression that our spiritual growth is all a matter of ascetical practice distort the whole meaning and the richness of our relationship with God.

We must learn to pray, then, in the deep inner core of our being. This is the wellspring of prayer, whether it be meditative, contemplative, liturgical or communal. Humans need external expression, but it has value as prayer only to the degree that it flows from the deep inner recesses of our being. I suggest that this was what Jesus meant when he taught us that when we pray we should go to our room, close the door and pray to the Father in secret (Mt. 6:6).

Prayer Of The Heart

Much has been written on what is called centering prayer, or prayer of the heart. Simply stated, this is merely a matter of leaving behind the turmoil of the surface and descending gently within ourselves, there to meet God. In that inner sanctuary words or even beautiful thoughts are unnecessary. It is simply a matter of standing before God in an attitude of openness and worship in the awareness that we are meeting him face to face.

There with God we gradually become attuned to the beauty that his presence brings to the inner temple that we are; that we become aware of the many ways he has graced us; that we begin to feel a surge of deep gratitude for all that he is and gives us. The peace of such an encounter little by little begins to move out from that center and calms the turmoil on the surface. The problems experienced in the outer self begin to subside because they are being treated at their roots. The leaves of a plant are not made to grow and become healthy by treating them directly but by feeding the plant at its roots.

Healing The Inner Self

A word should be added here about inner healing. We are very conscious today of the need for healing, not only of the illnesses of the body but even more of the wounds of our inner spirit. In the type of prayer that we have described, healing does imperceptibly take place. It can happen all the more by making our prayer for healing more explicit.

We can ask Jesus, the divine healer, to touch and heal those inner wounds we have suffered through life, or we can ask the Father and the Son to send the Holy Spirit to exercise his healing power within us. A verse of the Sequence of Pentecost comes to mind in which we pray to the Holy Spirit: "Wash clean the sinful soul, rain down your grace on the parched soul, and heal the injured soul. Soften the hard heart, cherish and warm the ice-cold heart, and give direction to the wayward."

Healing, under the divine touch, begins deep within but it does not remain there. Slowly and imperceptibly it reaches out to the surface of our being and begins to calm the tempests that blow there.

What is said here about healing is not intended to deny the power for healing that is contained in the prayer of a supporting community. It is only intended to stress that this is also a way to experience the healing power of God.

A Sense Of Humor

As we learn to live and pray more on this deep level, we can begin to develop a certain sense of humor about the vagaries of our outer self. We discover that even while we experience tension on the surface, as it wages its own battles, and even as we find ourselves very sin-prone, we can live in peace at the deep core of our being. We come to see that it is not what happens on the surface but what happens within that determines our true relationship with God.

The peace we discover is based on the same premise that Saint Paul invoked in Chapter 8 of Romans. He asks the question, "Who will separate us from the love of Christ?" Then after listing the many threats that we face, he concludes that nothing "will be able to separate us from the love of God that comes to us in Christ Jesus, our Lord" (Rom. 8:35-39). What Saint Paul is really saying is not that we are so strong in the love of Christ but that nothing can stop the flow of his love to us. And this flow of love occurs at the deep inner core of our being.

The Inner Self Of Others

Our main concern has been to point out the value and importance of discovering and living on the level of our real self. But before concluding, a word is in place about an important corollary to what we have been saying. It has to do with our relationship with others.

We live, not as isolated individuals, but in community with other people. For some this is in the family, for others in a religious community, for most relatedness is experienced in a situation of service of others. It is important that we apply the insight we have gained into ourselves to our understanding and acceptance of others.

Inevitably, in human relatedness we are not attracted to all to the same degree. We may be drawn strongly to some, others may be relatively easy to accept, if not to love. But we will meet, and sometimes live with, certain individuals that we find difficult. In fact, this appears to me more and more to be a universal experience. Nearly everyone has some one, or some ones, that present a real problem to them. I submit that no amount of asceticism will ever succeed in bridging this gap. It can be bridged only on the level that we have been discussing.

The Outer Source Of Trouble

We have to realize that the source of our difficulty with others is in their outer, superficial self. And that self, like our own, has been shaped by its own particular history, much of it beyond their control. That outer self is not the real person we are dealing with. He or she also has a deep inner self where the creative hand of God has produced goodness. In that inner self God dwells, redemption has been experienced, and it is a citadel of goodness and beauty. That inner self, like our own, is waiting to be freed. Its goodness needs to filter out to the surface and transform what we find unattractive there.

We must see ourselves as important instruments in setting that inner person free. We cannot do this if we persist in seeing that person only as a set of unattractive manifestations, any more than we ourselves can experience transformation by focusing on our outer self. We can do it only by seeking to discover the unique creation that person is and learning to love him or her on that level. Here too, little by little, healing occurs and the attitude applied to the inner person of the other begins to touch the surface self in the form of kindness, understanding, and acceptance.

3

Living With The Mystery Of God

When we begin to live a life of the Spirit, we have vivid dreams of what the journey will be like. We think that as time goes on our vision will become ever clearer until finally we will be complete master of the situation. We picture the path ahead as much like that of a mountain climber. The way might be steep and the slopes hazardous, but if we but persevere in our climb we will eventually stand at the peak of the mountain and feel the exhilaration of being master of all that we survey.

Different Lessons To Learn

Following the way of the Spirit, however, teaches us quite different lessons than we expected. We have to learn that in this path all our known images of progress and success fail to express the reality. What makes all such images inadequate is the fact that here victory is not a matter of conquest but of surrender. We have to come to see that learning the ways of God involves a great deal of unlearning. Most of all, it involves progressive growth in the art of living with mystery.

In no area of the life of the Spirit is this more true than in that which is most basic to it: our relationship with and our understanding of God. God is obviously the focal point and the source of all life in the Spirit. But how different is the God we eventually discover from the one we sought at the start!

Perhaps the most shattering experience of all is coming to realize that we do not possess God at all; rather he possesses us. Arriving at this point involves a process of learning, unlearning, and then learning all over again that keeps repeating itself as we come closer to being at home with the mystery that is God. John the Baptist described our experience perfectly when he said of Christ, "He must increase; I must decrease" (Jn. 3:30). Such is the strange paradox that we meet in our search for God.

A Beginner's Notion Of God

In order to describe our experience, we have to go back to a very early point of our life and reflect on the genesis of our notion of God. Our idea of God began as a name that we were taught as very small children. Perhaps he was a collection of names, each with its own connotations in our conditioned youthful minds. Such names as God, Father, Lord, Spirit, Jesus might have been among those by which we were taught to call him.

To the name of God, as well as to its variants, we attached a picture. Our pictures varied widely from person to person, depending upon what we had already instinctively associated with these names as a result of our experience. An obvious example of the variations on such pictures is found in the case of Father. Depending on our experience of our own father, our picture of God as Father could vary from a very loving image to a very severe one.

Equipped with such images of God, we moved little by little into the drama of our life. We grew physically, intellectually, and emotionally. Our experience of life gradually broadened as we moved forward to eventual adulthood.

As all these forms of growth were taking place, in all likelihood many of us did not mature proportionately in our concept of God. Unfortunately it is possible to go a long way in life carrying with us the same image of God that we learned as small children. As a result, it is easily possible to grow into adulthood with a very immature relationship with God. Thus, we can tend for a long time to experience religion as very much a formality, a matter of rigid duty and anything but a joyful experience. We may, in practice, be related to God as to one whom we fear more than love, and be more concerned with his punishments than with the gift of life that he holds out to us.

The Picture Begins To Change

Whatever the limitations of our individual word or image for God were, such is the wonder of

God's power that he can accomplish his purposes through them. At any rate, our awareness of God and his place in our life was strong and real enough that we were able to hear him calling us to a fuller life in him. Hopefully, we have already come to see the inadequacy of some of our former ideas of God and are growing to richer ones.

All of us have experienced in some degree the frustration of having failed to live up fully to what we might have thought of as our "contract" with God. No doubt most of us have come to some discovery that God's call is not a once-for-all thing, but is ever repeating itself in our life, summoning us to higher goals. Then we have begun to face the challenge of an ongoing conversion that will never end until the day we die. Out of all this, hopefully, we have come to feel that yearning that eventually possesses everyone who is sincere in his or her search, the desire to see the face of God.

The wonder of God's love and power is that he can and does lead us beyond those early, and often long-enduring, limited notions of him. For those who are sincerely striving for growth we offer the following reflections on the mystery of our God. For some, these thoughts might serve as a mirror in which to view their experience of God as they have already been through it. For others, they might be a help to greater courage in their continuing search for the hidden God. The reflections are grouped under certain aspects of the mystery of God that seem significant to this writer. They are suggested not only by his own experience but also that of those who have shared the fruits of their search with him.

A Mysterious God

An Invisible God

At first sight, it might seem strange that a God who is invisible should present any problem. After all, one of the earliest truths that we learned about God is the fact that we cannot see him. As we grow in our search for him, however, God's invisibility is something that we have to learn to cope with. As he becomes more real in our life we grow in the desire to somehow be able to grasp him. This was the great desire of Saint Teresa of Avila: "I want to see God." When God is only a name to us, even if we have given him a picture, we can accept the fact that we cannot see him. But the more personally he enters into our life the more his invisibility can become a cause of frustration.

What is more, we have to face the fact that the very pictures we have formed of God are so unreal that they must be discarded. From an unknown author of fourteenth century England we have a spiritual classic, popular again today, entitled "The Cloud of Unknowing." In it he elaborates in charming fashion the teaching of Pseudo-Dionysius that coming to know God is a process of unlearning what we think we have come to know about him.

The author says we must enter into the cloud of forgetting all that we thought we knew. Through a process of unknowing, we must enter into a cloud of darkness and, without images or words, come into communication with the God of light. This teaching is repeated again two centuries later by Saints John of the Cross and Teresa, and has been the teaching of all Christian tradition.

Everyone who sincerely seeks the Lord sooner or later is led into this cloud by the Lord himself. Even though it leads to a deeper and fuller knowledge of God, there is the element of death in accepting the fact that we cannot see the God whom we have come to desire so much.

C. S. Lewis expresses this experience in very graphic fashion: "Only God himself can let the bucket down to the depths in us. And, on the other side, he must constantly work as the iconoclast. Every idea of him we form, he must in mercy shatter. The most blessed result of prayer would be to rise thinking 'But I never knew before. I never dreamed . . . .' I suppose it was at such a moment that Thomas Aquinas said of all his own theology: 'It reminds me of straw'" (*Letters to Malcolm*, p. 82).

As in dealing with all the problems of the mystery of God, the reward of enduring this experience of darkness and death is great. The more we succeed in turning loose our limiting ideas and pictures of God, the more we enter the mystery of him who is all light.

An All Knowing God

Another experience of the mystery of God is coming to realize that nothing can be hidden from his eyes. Again, we are dealing with a truth about God that we learned to express in words very early in life. But as we move from the named and pictured God to a personal awareness of him, we can be bothered by the fact that he sees and knows us so completely. What happens is that a basic problem most of us have with ourselves gradually or suddenly becomes a problem in our relationship with God.

It is common knowledge that lack of self-acceptance is one of the most basic human conflicts. Because of an education that was often lacking in positive self-affirmation as well as the personal experience of sin and failure in our life, most of us do not have a very positive self-image. As a means of self-defense we often spend a great deal of time and emotional energy trying to hide our true self from others, and even from ourselves. We feel that if others were to know us as we really are they would not like us. To keep ourselves from being too discouraged, we try to avoid looking at the unpleasant things we see in ourselves. The result is the alienation from self that so often afflicts our contemporary society.

Since this experience is so real and so very personal to us, we easily project the problem on God himself. As we grow in the awareness of how deep and personal the love of the Lord for us is, we see ever more clearly the contrast between his holiness and our sinfulness. Since we have such a well developed habit of trying to hide, we instinctively try to hide even from God and from the rays of his love. We feel that if we really let ourselves be seen by him, he cannot really love us. So we engage in that most irra-

tional of all games, that of trying to shield ourselves from his sight. We find it difficult to pray in
peace because so much of our energy is devoted
to keeping him from seeing us as we are.

We are involved in another crisis in learning
the art of living with a God of mystery. Somehow,
by patient effort, we have to come to see and be
at peace with the fact that God never looks at us
in condemnation but that his look is a healing
look and the solution to the evil that we see so
clearly in ourselves. Again, the pain of struggling
with this problem can be great, but the joy of
experiencing his healing touch can be even
greater.

A Loving God

It might seem strange that coming to know
God as all loving should ever present any problem to us. After all, one of our most basic human
cravings is for love. We grasp for signs of love in
any form in which they present themselves. It
would seem, therefore, that coming to know God
as all loving would be a most welcome experience. But this is not always the case.

It is quite right to say that the Good News, in
the final analysis, is the fact that God really loves
us. This Good News is designed, in the plan of
God, to be the fullest possible answer to our
need for love. We can see this theoretically and
can really desire to know and experience his love
for us. But when it comes to letting ourselves receive this love we meet with many barriers. These
barriers are very much tied up with the poor
self-image mentioned in the previous section. Just

as we are afraid to let God see us, so we are afraid to let him really love us. So conscious are we of our own unworthiness that we tend to shield ourselves from the rays of God's love. Irrational as this is, it can be a very real experience for many.

Why is this so? For one thing we know intuitively that to let ourselves really receive God's love is going to demand that we enter on a serious path of *metanoia*, or conversion. It is not possible to let God's love touch us deep inside and still cling to the many forms of selfishness that remain so much a part of us. Closing ourselves off from his love is, therefore, largely a matter of our clinging to attachments that we are not quite ready to surrender to him. And as long as we remain unwilling to say a deep YES to God, the thought of his love for us will be a source of unrest rather than one of peace.

Another aspect of this fear of God's love is our reluctance to let God be what he says he is: a forgiving God. Much as we desire forgiveness for our sins, we are still afraid to receive it graciously. Perhaps this is a remnant of the age-old heresy of Pelagianism in us—clinging to the idea that we must save ourselves, or at least deserve that forgiveness.

Once more, we are engaged in a mere sham battle, but it can be very real on the level of experience. The very conflict that we feel is itself an invitation from God to a progressively more generous surrender of ourselves to him. Coping successfully with the problem leads us ultimately to the peace-giving knowledge that God's love for us and his forgiveness of our sins is based on nothing but that very love itself. We are indeed unworthy of his love and always will be. We must learn to accept that love as his free gift to us.

A God Who Calls Us, and Calls by Name

We come to another crucial aspect of our experience of God as we become more serious in our search for him. It is the awareness that God's call to us is not a once-for-all thing but something that is continually repeated and becomes ever more insistent.

We are touching here on what we usually think of as our vocation. Perhaps we have our ideas of that vocation neatly categorized as a general Christian vocation received at baptism, and as a vocation to the married, single, or religious life which we received at a point in time and that led us into one of these states.

If that is the limit of our notion of God's call, we are in for a rude awakening. Sooner or later we have to learn that those initial calls were only high points in what is a lifelong unfolding process. God's call is a challenge and invitation of every day and every moment. The closer we come to him the more clearly we should hear that call. We must develop an attitude like that taught by Eli to Samuel: "Speak, Lord, your servant is listening!" (1 Sam. 3:10)

In this, as in all processes of knowing God, we are involved in moving from a named, pictured, impersonal God to a God who is deeply personal. The more personal he becomes to us the more we see that he could never be content to call us only in a general way. He calls us by name, and he calls us each moment to open ourselves to his love and his gifts. He says to us what Jesus said to his disciples: "I no longer speak to you as slaves, for a slave does not know what his master is about. Instead, I call you friends, since I have made known to you all that I heard from the Father" (Jn. 15:15).

To the degree that we come to know God as eminently personal, as a God who calls each of us by name, the more we are led to open ourselves to that personal call of each moment. It becomes a bit scary, and we are reluctant to enter into such a personal relationship with him. But his call is leading us to just such a relationship. He is patient with us in our slowness to follow his call, but barring radical infidelity, he will lead us into such a relationship.

As we move toward such a personal relationship with God, we feel the anxieties of the risk involved. But as, little by little, we come closer to a deep surrender to him, we see that the darkness we have passed through is completely driven out by the light that floods us.

A God Who is Near

We speak now of one final aspect of God that takes some getting used to as we grow from naming and picturing God to an awareness of him as an eminently personal God. It is the growing awareness that he is not only a God of majesty who transcends all human experience, but also an immanent God who is so close to us that he enters into everything that becomes a part of our human life.

As long as, in our thought, God is in his highest heaven and pictured as a benign father surveying the human scene from afar, he is a safe God. There comes to mind the story of a wealthy lady who loved to pray Psalm 23: "The Lord is my shepherd, there is nothing I shall want," as all the while she was blissfully unconcerned about the poor people who sought her help. It is possible for any one of us to act like this in our own unique way so long as God is safely in his heaven.

Gradually, however, we come to see that our God is so concerned about all that happens to us that he is closer to us than we are to ourselves. The psalmist discovered this and described his experience in the beautiful 139th Psalm: "O Lord, you have probed me and you know me; you know when I sit and when I stand; you understand my thoughts from afar. My journeys and my rest you scrutinize, with all my ways you are familiar. Even before a word is on my tongue, behold, O Lord, you know the whole of it. Behind me and before me, you hem me in and rest your hand upon me" (Ps. 139: 1-5). God gave to his people Israel such an awareness of his immanent presence that they even at times attributed their own acts of malice to him. So deeply were they convinced that God was with them.

The awareness that God is right where we are calls for a deepening of our personal relationship with him. We can no longer be content with a purely formalistic and mechanical response to him but see the need to let him become a part of all that we are and do. We feel ourselves being called to a deeper life of communion with him through a growth in prayer that comes more and more to pervade our entire life.

There is a certain disturbing element in our growing awareness of how close our God is to us. There is the feeling of risk and uncertainty as well as a reluctance to face the implications of self-surrender that such an awareness brings. These growth pains are, as in all the other areas of deepening in the knowledge of God, a part of our experience of the night and the cross that are necessary if we are to see the light and know the power of his resurrection.

Discovering A God Of Mystery

We have discussed only some of the ways in which growth in the Spirit challenges us in our understanding of God. Other ways could be considered. But in each instance it is a matter of discovering a God of mystery and learning to live with that mystery. The God we come to know is so different and so much greater than the one we started out to seek. He becomes to us, a God to whom we cannot be content to assign a name and give a picture of, but a God who enters personally into our life and touches us deeply. It is no longer possible to deal with him in a formal or mechanical way, but rather we are challenged to enter into a very personal relationship with him. Untold wonders await the person who accepts, even if only hesitantly, this challenge.

Along the way, we have indicated that growing in awareness of the mystery of God involves pain, anxiety, and darkness. It should be pointed out that these symbols of death are part of the nights that the great spiritual masters speak about. And the nights are nothing but an experience of the cross that leads to the resurrection.

Our Surrender

By leading us through the cloud God accomplishes his designs in us. His desire is always to make us his own, to evoke a YES from us that is the surrender of our entire being to him. It is a surrender that we cannot make by our own will power but something that he alone can give in his own way and time.

One of the ways in which he prepares us to receive that gift is by purifying us in ways such as we have discussed. Through such purification we are stripped until we stand naked and needy before him. We are forced, as we come to know him better, to abandon our own plans for our salvation and say to him, "You alone are Savior."

Our relationship with God gradually sheds all formality and pretense and becomes a very consciously personal one. We begin to realize that our prayer is different without realizing how it happened. What has happened is that we have said a deeper YES to God, maybe without realizing it, and as a result what was once very formalistic is now deeply personal, and what was once clouded with darkness is now full of light.

In short, what really happens is that we catch a glimpse here on earth of what Saint Paul understood when he wrote, "Eye has not seen, ear has not heard, nor has it so much as dawned on man what God has prepared for those who love him" (1 Cor. 2:9).

The mystery, as well as the irony of it all, is that we will have to repeat the process all over again. Having gone through the night and welcomed the new light, we will have to be plunged again into darkness and await still another dawn. Such is the wonder of the God whom we seek.

4

Living With The Mystery Of Sin

When we walk seriously in the way of the Lord we must learn sooner or later to live in a world of mystery. This might sound like a trite statement because, after all, is not the Christian way of life based upon mystery? All the same, learning to live gracefully with mystery is not as simple as it would seem at first sight.

In the beginning of our serious strivings we tend to look upon the journey ahead, not as a path of mystery, but as a project that we undertake. We treat it as we would any other project, such as getting an education, running a business, or planning an outing. We determine the goals that we seek and try to establish them firmly in our minds. We single out the obstacles that we can foresee and try to identify them clearly. Then we search for the means that we can use to overcome the obstacles and attain the goals. We feel that while it may be a difficult path at times, it will only be a matter of time until everything falls neatly into place and we will have clear sailing ahead.

A Mystery To Be Lived

Such an approach may well be a practical way to enter into the way of the Spirit, and it might serve us well for a long time. But as we continue to walk the path, as the abrasions of life begin to wear us down, as disillusionment with ourselves makes itself felt and, most of all, as the Lord takes the direction of our life more into his own hands, such an approach becomes no longer adequate. The neatness of the project as we conceived it begins to cloud a bit, and gradually we must learn the truth of the statement: "Life is not a problem to be solved but a mystery to be lived."

Learning to live with mystery can become a crisis point in our spiritual striving. The core of the crisis is found in our reluctance to yield control of the task we have undertaken. We like so much to be in control. We yearn so much for the satisfaction we hope to feel when we have finally finished the project and solved the problem.

But in the world of mystery where the life of the Spirit is lived, this clinging tendency must clash headlong with the fact that spiritual growth is more a matter of surrender than of personal accomplishment. Little by little we must learn to turn loose our will to be in control and stand in awe with the helplessness of Christian humility before the God who seeks to be Lord of our lives. It sounds so simple and obvious, but failure to meet and cope with the crisis can doom us to living a bogus spiritual life or to a turning in on ourselves that can lead to the brink of despair.

The Mystery Of Sin

Learning to live with mystery has many dimensions. The particular aspect that I wish to discuss here is that of living with the mystery of sin, not as a theoretical reality but as it touches us personally.

When we begin our spiritual search we are quite aware that sin will be something to be dealt with. But because we are under the spell of idealism we feel that it will be only a temporary problem that will eventually be overcome. As time passes, however, and we experience those rough edges of life mentioned before, we come to the frightening awareness that sin is a far deeper and more personal reality than we ever dreamed of. We learn this not by anything that we hear or read but by the shattering experience of sin in our own person, if not by actions, at least by inclination.

In other words, we come to see what Saint Paul expressed in his letter to the Romans: "We know that the law is spiritual, whereas I am weak flesh sold into the slavery of sin. I cannot even understand my own actions. I do not do what I want to do but what I hate . . . . I know that no good dwells in me, that is, in my flesh; the desire to do right is there but not the power. What happens is that I do, not the good that I will to do, but the evil I do not intend" (Rom. 7:14-19).

Words Of Encouragement

Surely these words are given us by God, the author of Scripture, not only for the truth they state but also for the encouragement they would give to so many people through the ages who would duplicate the experience of Saint Paul. Somehow, we can feel more at ease with our own experience when we realize that Saint Paul, that great lover and apostle of Jesus, had the same experience and the same reaction.

As we sense more and more these contradictory forces of good and evil within us, we easily and naturally tend to become preoccupied with the reality of sin within us. This preoccupation can lead us to the point where we even question the sincerity of all our ideals and strivings. It also leads to various forms of inner conflict.

On the human level, because most of us tend to question our own worth to begin with, we can find ourselves feeling a real fear. On a deeper spiritual level, we can feel what the spiritual masters speak of as a sense of dread.

This dread is the natural result of our clarity of vision of the holiness of God and the insistence of his call in our life on the one hand, and the deep awareness of sin on the other. Sin is now seen, not as a theoretical force that can threaten us, but as something that is deeply rooted in our own person. In this experience of contradiction is found much of the raw material of the dark nights and of the process of purification.

At A Crucial Point

In the darkness of this dread, peace seems to be elusive. We crave it, but it seems to be out of our reach. We want so desperately to pray, but there seems to be an impenetrable wall between us and God. We tend to question the truth and sincerity of all our previous experience. We are at a crucial point in our search to see the face of the living God.

This experience becomes very real at one time or another to everyone who tries to walk in the way of the Lord. As we said, it can be an experience of the dark nights of which the classical writers speak. But it is not perceived as such, making the night even darker. It is also an experience of the Passion aspect of the Paschal Mystery, but on our feeling level it seems to be a living contradiction of that same Paschal Mystery.

The Dynamics Of The Struggle

Let us look for a moment at the factors and dynamics of this struggle with the mystery of sin. Even though this is a conflict that cannot be solved by reason but only by living experience, still an understanding of the factors involved can be helpful in learning to live with the mystery.

Sin is a reality in everyone's life. Most of us waste a lot of energy trying to wish it away and in dreaming of an angelic existence. This is a manifestation of our controlling tendency, our desire to one day have the satisfaction of saying to ourselves, "I have gained the victory."

We should know better, of course. After all, the whole mystery of incarnation and redemption, so central to our faith, is essentially predicated on the reality of universal sin. Sacred Scripture repeatedly reminds us that none of us is exempt. Especially direct and unequivocal are the words of Saint John: "If we say, 'We are free of the guilt of sin,' we deceive ourselves; the truth is not to be found in us . . . . If we say, 'We have never sinned,' we make him a liar and his word finds no place in us" (1 Jn. 1:8, 10).

We have all heard these and similar words in Scripture numberless times, and we readily give assent to the truth of them. They are safe words as long as they are "out there," theoretical. But like so many of the points of revelation, when it comes to inserting myself into the picture, acknowledging that I am involved, we tend to balk. It is easy to nod assent when we hear, "All are sinners." It is even easy to agree that I am a sinner when it is a theoretical statement.

But when I find myself having to admit that I have sinned just now, specifically, and at a time when my vision is so clear of what I am called to be, then it is difficult. The neatness of my theoretical acceptance blurs into a painful sense of guilt — a guilt that is usually more directed to myself than to God. I am then confronted with the painful experience of living with the existential mystery of sin.

Looking For An Answer

When we find ourselves in this situation we want so much to find an answer. Because we want the answer to come from ourselves, we search through the data of our experience and knowledge for a solution to the dilemma. But such a search is doomed to failure because we are looking for a way to resolve the matters ourselves. Again, it is our controlling tendency at work. But, alas, there is no answer that can come from us. We are dealing with a mystery, but we are trying to cope with it as if it were a problem.

The pain of this experience is all the greater as we are faced with the horror of the wounds of sin within and gradually become aware that all the answers we have known, and all the means we have used before will not meet this situation. We have reached the crisis point mentioned before.

At this point we run the risk of turning in on ourselves and in total frustration moving to the verge of despair. I fear that some very sincere persons cease to strive earnestly to live spiritually because of a simple inability to cope with the contradiction they feel within themselves. They have come to a deep knowledge of their own unworthiness without having grown correspondingly in awareness of the meaning of redemption.

A Giant Step Forward

The crisis point need not, however, lead us to introspection and despair. Like all crises, this one can also be an occasion of a giant step forward. Inherent in the experience is the call from God to surrender to him and let him be to us what he really is — Lord and Savior.

Oddly enough, we are so afraid of this type of surrender. Even though we know that all things are already in his hands, that we cannot escape his providence which governs our life, we find it so hard to ratify by a deeply spoken "Yes" what already is the true state of things. It seems we cannot reason ourselves to this "Yes" or say it by the brute force of our own will power.

We have to wait until God gives us the grace to say it from the core of our being. If and when he gives us his grace, we discover the tremendous and awe-inspiring truth that all things are his gift, and we learn one of the deepest lessons in living with mystery in our life. Also, our "Yes" is the closest thing to adoration we have ever experienced.

Accepting Redemption

It seems, then, that our real challenge in coping with the mystery of sin is that of deeply and personally accepting redemption and learning to live, not as self-sufficient people, but as redeemed people. It can be more than a little humiliating to realize that we can come so late to an internalized awareness of this simple truth that was one of the earliest we learned to express in words.

It would be comforting if, at this point, I could give a formula for learning this truth in a personal way. Even as I write this there is the wish that I could give such a formula. But I am afraid that part of the mystery is that there is no such formula. If we were to try to formulate a solution, we would be once again trying to solve as a problem what is really a mystery that we have to live out in God's own way and time.

The greatest security and comfort we can find is in clinging to the belief that God who calls us also gives us the grace to walk in his way. If we remain sincere in our struggle for growth, God will see to it that we will graduate from the world of problems into the world of mystery. There will be darkness, uncertainty and doubt, but he will reveal to us his way, often only in hindsight. We will come to know the joy of living in total dependence upon him who has pledged his fidelity to those who seek him with a sincere heart. This discovery will be like the dawning of a brilliant spring after a long, hard winter.

The words that instinctively come to mind as a fitting way to end these reflections are the words of God to his people in a time of dark distress more than five centuries before the coming of Christ:

> But now, thus says the Lord, who created you, O Jacob, and formed you, O Israel: Fear not, for I have redeemed you; I have called you by name; you are mine. When you pass through the water, I will be with you; in the rivers you shall not drown. When you walk through fire, you shall not be burned; the flames shall not consume you. For I am the Lord, your God, the Holy One of Israel, your savior" (Is. 43:1-3).

5

When I Am Weak
Then I Am Strong

Scripture reveals two things very clearly: 1) that God is all holy, and 2) that all humans are sinners. In the account of Isaiah's vocation the seraphim cried to one another, "Holy, holy, holy is the Lord of hosts, the earth is filled with his glory!" (Is. 6:3) Saint John tells us, "If we say we are free of the guilt of sin, we deceive ourselves; the truth is not to be found in us" (1 Jn. 1:8).

The contrast between these two overwhelming realities provides the arena for the spiritual combat that we are involved in. If we even begin to grasp the meaning of these two facts and the contrast between them we cannot help being moved to a certain fear. If we grasp them in their full implications our fear can verge on terror. We find ourselves caught in the vise of what, to human understanding, are irreconcilable opposites. From the human viewpoint there is no answer to the dilemma that these two opposites pose. Human judgment would lead only to darkness and despair.

The Mystery That Unites Opposites

At the heart of Christian revelation there is a mystery that brings these two opposites together and provides an answer to the dilemma they create. It is the overarching mystery of the death and resurrection of Jesus Christ. This mystery contains the answer, but learning it is a slow process. It is so tied up with the struggle for spiritual growth that it forms its very web and fabric.

That God is all holy is something that we come to see in a personal way only by the mysterious process of faith. Coming to see it as the dazzling light that it is does not follow the norms of rational thought. Rather, it is an insight that grows into a person through exposure to that light until it becomes an intuition that transcends the rational. This intuition can come only through much prayer over a long period of time.

We Are Sinners

That we are sinners is closer to home. Awareness of it comes to us through our daily personal experience. We would have to be blind not to see it.

A broader scope for considering this mystery of holiness-sinfulness is another biblical concept of power and weakness. Sin is but the most dramatic and baffling manifestation of weakness.

There are others that are closely related and that deserve consideration. This chapter is an attempt at a prayerful reflection on the divine and human mystery of power working through weakness as it is experienced by humans who are also believing Christians.

Forms Of Weakness

Let us look at some of the ways that we experience weakness. These play on all of us in varying degrees at different times. Each experience has its own impact and all together have the cumulative effect of showing us how very limited we are. There may be times along the way when we think we have finally learned all there is to know about weakness. Then something happens to make us realize that we still have much to learn. Such is the pattern of human and spiritual growth in understanding.

We should begin with the obvious, which is physical weakness and limitation. Many of us are conditioned by our upbringing to feel that we can accomplish anything we set our mind to. But along the way we have to face the fact that this is an illusion spawned by an ambitious culture. By piling work on work we may have to learn that the body has its limitations, and it lets us know by flashing the signal of ill health.

If our fixation on our presumed strength is deep enough this discovery can be rather traumatic and challenge our very ego and sense of worth. For others, physical illness may be a lifetime companion. Living with this amid people who are healthy presents another form of challenge. Then there is the aging process that is so built in to the human journey that no one escapes it. Whatever form it takes, the fact of physical weakness cannot be denied. Ultimately it must be accepted as real and adjusted to.

Emotional Limitation

Then there is the less definable form of weakness that we shall call emotional limitation. This may come in the form of an innately weak emotional structure, or it may be the result of struggles engaged in. To the one who experiences this kind of weakness, it is very real. Sometimes it may take the form of free-floating anxiety, the source of which defies all effort to pinpoint. It is not something that we can diagnose as we do an ailment of the body, but the victim can suffer intensely from it. Many such emotional struggles are shared in common, while others are as varied and unique as the individual. Through the experience of our emotional limitations each of us must eventually learn another lesson of weakness.

Relational Weakness

Let us single out another form of weakness and call it relational. I refer to that broad area of communication with one another. It may apply to relationships with others in community, family, work, or the many other settings where lives touch. As the result of sharing the inner struggles of many other people, it is a growing conviction of this writer that nearly everyone has at least one person that he or she finds difficult. It seems as if this is a common ground on which we all meet. It can be a very troublesome thing. All efforts to remedy the conflict seem to fail, and we are forced to accept a situation that we have to learn to live with. One who experiences this needs no convincing that it is a form of weakness that produces its own feeling of helplessness.

Sin — The Mystery Of Iniquity

Other forms of human weakness and limitation could be singled out, but I suspect they would be but variations of those already mentioned. Let us go on to look at what must be the most baffling of all forms of human weakness and that is sin. Every human being must come sooner or later to know the meaning of Saint John's words already quoted: "If we say we are free of the guilt of sin, we deceive ourselves and the truth is not to be found in us" (1 Jn. 1:8). In the same place Saint John goes on to say, "If we say we have never sinned, we make him a liar and his word finds no place in us" (1 Jn. 1:10). What the Scripture tells us so emphatically must be discovered by everyone in a personal way sooner or later.

Scripture calls sin the mystery of iniquity. It is a mystery that will always defy adequate understanding. The mystery of it cannot be learned by study; it can only be experienced in a way that makes it all the more mysterious. If sin is seen in the context of the awesome holiness of God, then the real depth of its mystery is felt.

It is here, I believe, that the deepest experiences of the mystics take place. The darkness they speak of comes in large part from seeing God from the felt position of sinfulness. Their growth to fullness of life in God is the process of the light that is God overcoming the darkness that is sin.

Contradiction

What makes sin so utterly baffling to one whose faith is strong is its element of contradiction. I refer not so much to the obvious contradiction between the holiness of God and sin, but rather to the feeling one has when he or she knows so deeply the holiness of God and the powerful yearning of the heart to be in his light; knows also by gradual discovery that one's path has been and is flooded with the gifts of God's love. With this overwhelming awareness one sees that sin is not only still a possibility but a reality.

Sin appears as the ultimate contradiction not only of what one stands for but of what one has actually experienced. I believe it is precisely this feeling that the saints express when they seem to say such negative things about themselves. Of all the forms of human weakness this must be the most painful.

At the same time sin presents our greatest challenge to enter fully into the mystery of power in weakness as it is found in the passion and resurrection of Jesus. When confronted with the mystery of sin, human reason fails completely to provide any adequate answers. But by faith we can come to see that hidden in the very experience of sin is the key to open the way for God's own power to do its work in us.

The Incarnation And Weakness

We turn now to the mystery of Jesus, seeking light on the meaning of weakness in God's plan. The mystery of Jesus is one of weakness. We do not begin to grasp the implications of Saint John's simple statement in the prologue of his gospel: "The Word became flesh and made his dwelling among us" (Jn. 1:14). Since the time of the gospel men and women have probed the implications of this, and they have not been exhausted. Each of us has some awareness of what it means that God became man, but there is so much more to be learned. If we ever come to understand the incarnation we will finally know the mystery of God and that of our own life.

All through history people have had difficulty balancing the human and the divine in Jesus. Intermittently, strong attention has been given to the human in him, especially at times of universal human suffering such as the Black Death. But for the most part, such careful effort has been made to safeguard the divine in him that the human has tended to be neglected. As a result we have inherited an inadequate appreciation of how fully he entered into the human condition. There is great need for greater discovery here.

The Infancy Of Jesus

The helplessness of the infancy of Jesus speaks its own message to simple hearts. It is perhaps here that the faith of the Church is at its best as people contemplate the infant of Bethlehem. Before the crib, the faithful do not need a theology to explain what they see. It may not be as easy to keep the message clear in other aspects of his life.

Interpreters of the Scripture tell us that the whole meaning of the temptations of Jesus in the desert is tied up with the mystery of weakness. In the three specific forms the temptations take, Jesus is being asked to by-pass the human experience and use only the divine. In each instance Jesus rejects the temptation and stays firmly on the path of human weakness to which the Father has called him. Does this not remind us of the ways in which we wish to be more divine, or at least angelic, in our striving for the realization of our ideals?

The Eucharist

Think of the Eucharist. It conforms so well to the entire pattern of the incarnation. Having lived his life on earth, experiencing all things that other humans do besides sin, Jesus comes to the end of his earthly life. He seeks a way in which he might remain even while leaving. He wishes his act of total self-giving out of love, so soon to be made, to be present to those whom he would redeem.

How does he do this? He takes the frail elements of bread and wine "which earth has given and human hands have made" and makes them the medium of his continued presence among his redeemed people. He takes a form that is even weaker than the flesh and blood that is his humanity. Even today, twenty centuries later, he says to us when the bread of the Eucharist is placed in our hands, "See, I come to you in this way so that you will not be afraid."

Each time we learn something of how God does not need strong things to support his power. It is no wonder that God's people are drawn, as if by instinct, to the Eucharist. In it they find contact with the all holy God even as they are reassured about the weakness of their human state.

The Passion Of Jesus

In the passion of Jesus, the meaning of weakness is revealed with full force. His life was so human that, like all other human lives, it would come to an end. The will of the Father for the salvation of his people was unfolding in his beaten and wounded flesh. As Jesus experienced it, his passion and death came to him through the convergence of very human forces motivated by malice. His agony during his passion reflects how very vulnerable he was and in how fully human a way he felt his passion.

The full impact of the words of Saint Paul comes home to us as we look at Jesus in his passion:

> Though he was in the form of God, he did not deem equality with God something to be grasped

at. Rather, he emptied himself and took the form of a slave, being born in the likeness of men. He was known to be of human estate, and it was thus that he humbled himself, obediently accepting even death, death on a cross (Phil. 2:6-8).

The Resurrection

If the story ended there, we would still be left without an answer. But the whole wonder of the Christian mystery is found in the continuation of Saint Paul's text:

Because of this, God highly exalted him and bestowed on him the name above every other name, so that at Jesus' name every knee must bend in the heavens, on the earth, and under the earth, and every tongue proclaim to the glory of God the Father: Jesus Christ is Lord! (Phil. 2:9-11)

Beyond death there is resurrection; beyond defeat is victory. Weakness itself becomes the vehicle of that victory. The greatest of all God's works is accomplished, not in a blaze of glory, but in the ultimate symbol of weakness that is death. Because of this, all those who believe in him can live in hope that their own victory is possible. This not through strength but through weakness. Again Saint Paul instructs us:

May he enlighten your innermost vision that you may know the great hope to which he has called you, the wealth of his glorious heritage to be distributed among the members of the church, and the immeasurable scope of his power in us who believe. It is like the strength he showed in raising

Christ from the dead and seating him at his right hand in heaven (Eph. 1:18-20).

Saint Paul On Power In Weakness

After his dramatic conversion to Christ on the road to Damascus, Saint Paul grew to a tremendously deep awareness of Christ in his life. His letters reveal a total preoccupation with the death and resurrection of Christ. He speaks often of the Christ who died, but rarely without adding that he rose again. He speaks also of our share in the dying of Christ, but it is always that we may live with him.

When he explains Christian baptism, and therefore what being a Christian is all about, he writes: "Are you not aware that all we who are baptised into Christ Jesus were baptised into his death? Through baptism into his death we were buried with him, so that, just as Christ was raised from the dead by the glory of the Father, we too might live a new life" (Rom. 6:3-4). It is clear that for Paul, a Christian is called to live the death and resurrection of Christ.

For Saint Paul, this was not an empty formula. In his life as an apostle he met the practical implications of it. Among them, he devotes a great deal of attention to the experience of human weakness in its various forms.

The Classic Text

The most classic of all his texts on this must be the one found in the twelfth chapter of Second

Corinthians. He is defending his ministry as an apostle. He gives a long list of the sufferings he has endured in pursuit of that ministry, and then he goes so far as to boast of visions and revelations of the Lord. At the end of this account he writes:

> As to the extraordinary revelations, in order that I might not become conceited I was given a thorn in the flesh, an angel of Satan to beat me and keep me from getting proud. Three times I begged the Lord that this might leave me. He said to me: "My grace is enough for you, for in weakness power reaches perfection." And so I willingly boast of my weaknesses instead, that the power of Christ might rest upon me. Therefore, I am content with weakness, with mistreatment, with distress, with persecutions and difficulties for the sake of Christ; for when I am powerless, it is then that I am strong (2 Cor. 12:7-10).

What a marvellous text to reassure us in our experience of weakness! We are told that it is not only all right to be weak, but that weakness is a necessary condition for the full power of God to work in us. This text leads us far beyond our rational judgment and instinctive feelings to a faith view of weakness.

Another Approach

Earlier in the same letter Saint Paul takes another approach to the same question. Here he is speaking of his mission to preach the gospel. He writes:

> This treasure we possess in earthen vessels, to make it clear that its surpassing power comes from

God and not from us. We are afflicted in every way possible, but we are not crushed; full of doubts, we never despair. We are persecuted but never abandoned; we are struck down but never destroyed. Continually we carry about in our bodies the dying of Jesus so that in our bodies the life of Jesus may also be revealed. While we live we are constantly being delivered to death for Jesus' sake, so that the life of Jesus may be revealed in our mortal flesh (2 Cor. 4:7-11).

We all share in some way in the same mission to bear the Good News to others. As we fulfill this mission we are constantly made aware that we do so with so much personal frailty. Even as we speak the message it can strike fire in our hearts, reminding us of how poorly we ourselves live the message. It is reassuring that the great apostle felt as we do. He shows us the awesome fact that the very frailty of the instrument enables the power of God to stand out all the more clearly.

God Uses Weak Instruments

In his first letter to the Corinthians, Saint Paul stresses the way God uses weak instruments to do his work. He is writing this letter to confront many abuses in the Church at Corinth. After painting a huge backdrop about the wisdom and folly of the cross he writes:

Brothers, you are among those called. Consider your situation. Not many of you are wise, as men account wisdom; not many are influential; and surely not many are well-born. God chose those whom the world considers absurd to shame the wise; he singled out the weak of this world to shame the strong. He chose the world's lowborn and despised, those who count for nothing, to reduce to nothing those who were something; so that mankind can do no boasting before God. God it is who has given you life in Christ Jesus. He has made him our wisdom and also our redemption. This is just as you find it written, "Let him who would boast, boast in the Lord" (1 Cor. 1:26-31).

It seems that Saint Paul often felt the need to remind his disciples where the source of their strength was. Was this because he knew weakness and limitation so well? Was it because he had to deal with people like ourselves, who so want to think we must be worthy and capable of doing it all ourselves? Whatever the reason, he makes the point again to the Ephesians:

I repeat, it is owing to God's favor that salvation is yours through faith. This is not your own doing, it is God's gift; neither is it a reward for anything you have accomplished, so let no one pride himself on it (Eph. 2:8-9).

The message of Saint Paul on the power of God working through weakness is most insistent. No doubt his conviction on this point was born of two things. During hours of prayer he had come to know the all holy God and the power he displayed through Jesus. He also found himself so immersed in the human condition that he had to find an answer. He found it, and expressed it in his amazing formula: "I willingly boast of my weaknesses that the power of Christ may rest upon me . . . . For when I am powerless, it is then that I am strong" (2 Cor. 12:9-10). Fortunately, he has left his insight for us to ponder for our instruction and inspiration.

Weakness, The Raw Material Of Purification

For as long as we live we will never get over the temptation to want to control our lives and become the strong persons we want to be. We will never outgrow the yearning to feel the satisfaction that we have gained the victory. But if we ever get to the point where we think this has happened, it is a sign we have gone astray along the way. The awareness of our own inadequacies must increase rather than decrease. In the very experience of weakness is the raw material of our purification.

If, to our experience, we can gradually bring the acceptance that Saint Paul came to, we will have found the key to holiness. We, too, need to become content with weakness and come to the conviction that "when I am powerless, it is then that I am strong." Any other way is an illusion.

We can see in Mary the perfect embodiment of what we have been discussing. Through her constant pondering of the Old Testament Scriptures she found her true place before God. She expressed this so beautifully in her song of praise at the time of the incarnation:

My being proclaims the greatness of the Lord, my spirit finds joy in God my savior. For he has looked upon his servant in her lowliness; all ages to come shall call me blessed" (Lk. 1:46-48).

6

Prayer Of The Imperfect

Our age is one that is often marked with confusion and dark omens, even to the point that some are tempted to think that God has abandoned his people to the spirit of this world. But as if the Spirit of God wishes to remind us that he is still with us, we are sometimes surprised by remarkable evidence of his presence.

Surely one of the most striking of these signs is the resurgence in our day of an interest in and a desire to pray. As evidence of this we need only recall the enthusiastic response given by so many to the liturgical renewal, the many prayer groups that meet regularly across the country, and even the interest in what so recently was thought of as a bit old-fashioned—contemplation. Perhaps the fact that these signs caught many of us by surprise is just another evidence of how little we had come to trust in the presence of the Holy Spirit with God's people.

What This Means

As one who has been surprised at and glad-
dened by this revival of interest in prayer, I have
reflected upon what all of this means. First of all,
I believe it means that a desire to pray was
never absent in the heart of the believing Christian. I believe this means that what we learned
from childhood on about prayer did fall on the
good soil of faith and took deep root. I refuse to
believe that we are only now learning to pray.
The fact that we have a past history of prayer is
all to our advantage as we try to make good use
of the new approaches given us today.

Secondly, and more importantly, I believe the
renewal of interest in prayer is the work of the
Holy Spirit in the Church. Just when so many
were beginning to feel unequal to the task of
Christian living in the modern world, the Spirit
wishes to teach us dramatically that meeting· such
a challenge is not within the power of people but
is the work of God.

In other words, it seems to me that the
prayer movement is a call from the Holy Spirit to
deeper conversion and openness to God that was
ever required of us before. The Scriptures had
told us this all along, but somehow we needed to
face our own poverty in all its starkness before
we were even capable of facing the truth.

A Particular Aspect Of Prayer

Much could be said about the implications of
the renewed prayer interest that we are witnessing

today, and it would all reveal deep insights into the way of God with his people. However, my concern in this chapter is with a particular aspect of the experience of prayer that has intrigued me for some time. It is this: How are we to relate truly and deeply to God in prayer, not in the ideal state of the perfect man or woman (that is easy), but as weak, sinful, often confused and disturbed human beings.

My preoccupation with this dimension of prayer has grown out of my own efforts at deeper prayer at a time when awareness was growing of how very complex and imperfect we still remain even after many years of effort at prayer. It is with a feeling that my own experience will strike a sympathetic chord in the hearts of many that I here endeavor to spell out my own reflections on this problem and hopefully some pointers to a solution.

An Implicit Attitude About Prayer

To set the scene for these reflections, I think we should begin by drawing something of a picture of what has probably been the implicit attitude of many of us about prayer. Much of our instruction and reading on prayer has dealt with prayer in its ideal state. For example, we have learned of the beauty of prayer, the ideal expression it should take, the way it should be experienced by the person who is perfectly and ideally in communion with God. Even prayer formularies that we learned used, for the most part, ideal language in the expression of our sentiments of God.

True, this is not all that we were taught. Even the most rudimentary knowledge of the ways of prayer would have conveyed some idea of the extensive treatment the masters give of such things as dryness, sadness, and the temptation to abandon prayer. But I think it would be true to say that many of us, while knowing a good deal intellectually about the difficulties of prayer, developed a dominant impression of prayer as being the ideal expression of an ideal relationship with God. Perhaps this simple fact is the culprit that haunts us as we often experience the frustration and sense of helplessness as we try to coax our imperfect selves into communion with God in prayer. It is with this imperfect self at prayer that we are here concerned.

The Perfect Person At Prayer

It is easy to conceptualize the perfect person in the act of prayer. Such a one would be a prototype of the fully developed, well integrated person whose nature some of us have studied in scholastic philosophy. Such a one, as we visualize him or her, would have no difficulty in moving gently and easily into a state of prayer. This person would be perfectly at peace, and all foreign distractions and concerns would be alien to such a one. Furthermore, with this person's well integrated faculties, he or she would know intuitively that the God being confronted is that most attractive, loving, and loveable God that is revealed to us by Scripture and so clearly defined by philosophy.

Even though such people would know that they are creatures, yes, even imperfect creatures, there would be no coloration of fear attached to this because there would be the peaceful awareness that this is as it should be. There would be the calm discovery of their true place before God and the ensuing peace of knowing that the good and all holy God accepts his creatures for what they are without accusation or condemnation. Prayer with all this clear-sighted awareness would be a spontaneous outpouring of the human spirit to the heart of God and the calm, peaceful experience of acceptance by a good and loving God.

Such a picture of the state of prayer is bound to be attractive and desirable. The sad thing is that, in practice, we tend to think of prayer as authentic only when experienced in this ideal form. Such an attitude fails to take into account the fact that human nature, when embodied in an existential person, never exists in perfect form. Therefore, to dream of our experience of prayer as that of a perfect creature in communion with the perfect God is to invade the world of fantasy and the non-existent.

A Quite Different Picture

When you and I try to enter into prayer we usually present quite a different picture than the one which we just considered. True, there may be times when we may be able to approximate that experience. Fortunately for us, we do have those moments of respite when we can feel something of the comfort and peace of praying. But it seems that more often, indeed for long periods at a time, we seem to have quite a different experience of prayer.

On a given occasion, I may approach prayer as a very worried person. There is trouble in the family or in my religious community. Some personal relationship has gone awry and I do not know quite how to cope with it. Obviously, my prayer that day is not going to be that of the ideal person.

Another day I go to prayer as a very anxious person. Perhaps I am facing a radical transition in my place of residence or my work, and I am not all sure I have the wherewithal to make the transition gracefully and successfully. Again, my prayer is not going to be that of the ideal person in a perfect state.

Still another time I go to prayer plagued with a deep sense of guilt. Perhaps I have not been true to my ideals to a very humiliating degree. I have difficulty in forgiving myself, much less accepting the forgiveness of God. Because I am not reconciled with myself, all that I know about the goodness and mercy of God seems unreal. I look to God and he seems to be turning away or frowning at me. If I persist in dreaming of prayer as genuine only in the ideal state, I am plunged all the more into depression and a sense of hopelessness.

These are merely examples drawn from the many possible distorted feelings that all of us bring to prayer many times. In fact, such experiences may at times seem so common that the fleeting experiences of peaceful prayer appear as rare as an oasis in the desert.

The Contrast Between Hope And Reality

By now, the aspect of prayer that I am addressing myself to must be crystal clear. Most of us are persons who desire intensely to pray, and yet we face the radical contrast that exists between our dreamed hope of prayer and the real state in which we find ourselves. We are caught directly in a bind that requires a decision.

We must either accept stoically that much if not most of the time we are doomed to failure in prayer. Or else we must adjust our idea of what it is to pray and search for means of relating to God as imperfect, sinful and often confused human beings. In the mere statement of the case I thing we sense intuitively where the answer must be sought. And yet the mere stating of it does not solve the problem. The question still remains: How can I become a person of prayer in those many times when I feel so incapable of it?

Realistic Psychological Insight

As we look for an answer to this question, I would like to direct attention first to what I would term realistic psychological insight. One of the most heartening developments of our day is the integration of sound psychological principles with the science of spiritual life. The stormy history of psychology from the time of Freud to the present need not concern us here. Suffice it to say that as a result of the revolution Freud began, attention has been increasingly directed not just to human nature, but to that nature as it exists in its manifold subjects that we are.

At first, the findings of psychology were taken as a threat to the integrity of the person as a spiritual being. But gradually we have come full circle to accepting the fact that existential man and woman are real, that they are here to stay, and that revealed truth applies to them in their real state. Thus, we are able to find light on our question from psychology that would not have been as possible a few years ago.

I Bring Myself To Prayer

Practically, in the area of prayer, we must simply accept the fact that the only person I can bring to prayer here and now is the person I am here and now. That we should be burdened with the problems we have discussed above on occasion, or even frequently, must be taken as a matter of course. Even though we may have to admit that we have brought some of those states upon ourselves, this is still the only me that I have at the moment. I cannot, by waving a magic wand, change the imperfect, sinful, confused me into an ideal, well integrated me that is perfectly ready for ideal, peaceful prayer.

This is not to say that I should not seek, in the struggle of prayer, for means of improving the me that I might bring to prayer in the future. But for now this is the real me and the only me that can possibly enter into prayer. This is a hard, cold fact that any effort to disregard will only accentuate. Such an attitude is a great step to self-acceptance in each here and now situation, and such self-acceptance is an indispensable condition for truly believing in God's acceptance of us at all times.

Applying The Principles Of Faith

Once we have faced and accepted the human reality of the situation, we need to apply the clear principles of faith to the problem of how to pray in our imperfect state. Sacred Scripture abounds in the assurance that God accepts us always as we are. To give a few examples:

> As a father has compassion on his children, so the Lord has compassion on those who fear him. For he knows how we are formed; he remembers that we are dust (Ps. 103:13-14).
> People who are healthy do not need a doctor; sick people do. I have come to call sinners, not the self-righteous (Mk. 2:17).
> My grace is enough for you, for in weakness power reaches perfection (2 Cor. 12:9).

Most of all, in search for an answer to the problem we have been discussing, I would like to call attention to a text that one who tries to pray cannot meditate upon enough. It is in the eighth chapter of Saint Paul's letter to the Romans.

> The Spirit too helps us in our weakness, for we do not know how to pray as we ought; but the Spirit

himself makes intercession for us with groanings that cannot be expressed in speech. He who searches hearts knows what the Spirit means, for the Spirit intercedes for the saints as God himself wills (Rom. 8:26-27).

In Touch With Reality

As we reflect on these words of Saint Paul, we feel instinctively that he is in touch with the reality that we know so well. According to our preconceived idea of the perfect person at prayer, we would imagine that Saint Paul did not know the problems that we experience, that prayer would have come easy to him. Yet, he seems here to be expressing the attitude of a man who knows the frustrations of certain efforts at prayer.

Yet he assures us that there is more to the situation than that we are trying to pray as imperfect human beings. He opens up the tremendous view of life in the Spirit. He assures us that when we cannot pray as we would like, we should remember that the Spirit is with us and that the Spirit's precise function is to pray with and for us, even to the point of formulating in words these inexpressible deep feelings of our heart. As if he is aware that he is speaking to people who might miss the obvious, he says, "God who knows everything in our hearts knows perfectly well what he means."

How comforting this text should be to those who become discouraged in their efforts at prayer, to those who tend to become more preoccupied with the awareness of human limitation than with the presence of the Spirit. What a realistic light it throws on prayer in the human condition.

An Act Of Our Will

Another attitude that might help us in dealing with this very human problem is an awareness of what belonging to God, clinging to him really involves. It is an act of our will, and our will is not just that active force within us that seems so often to lead us in the wrong direction. Much more basically, the will is the core force of our being which gives us our basic orientation. This will can be, and I think usually is, deeply rooted in the desire to cling to God even when superficially we are being pulled in every contrary direction. This very longing for God is itself a prayer to be understood in the light of Saint Paul's text: "The Spirit himself expresses our plea in a way that could never be put into words."

This chapter has posed a question that touches all of us in a most personal way: how to work at becoming persons of prayer, not as perfect human beings, but as the imperfect creatures that we are. I hope these thoughts will evoke other insights in the minds of readers, encouraging them to continue through darkness, doubt, and frustration to become persons of prayer in our imperfect human condition.

May all of us experience the reality of Saint Paul's exhortation to the Philippians:

Dismiss all anxiety from your minds. Present your needs to God in every form of prayer and in peti-

tions full of gratitude. Then God's own peace,
which is beyond all understanding, will stand guard
over your hearts and minds, in Christ Jesus (Phil.
4:6-7).

7

Prayer As Listening

Much that we have learned and experienced tends to make us think that prayer must always involve some kind of activity. From early childhood we were taught to *say* prayers. Our experience of liturgy has included a great deal of words, actions, and posture. Even what most of us were taught about meditation has stressed that we be active in concentrating on points and turning away distractions and drowsiness. As a result, many people never get over the impression that unless their time of prayer is filled with intense activity it is a failure.

God Is Where We Are

If we are to develop a truly prayerful spirit we must get beyond such limited and often mechanical notions as these. Prayer is not a device we use in order to lay hold of God and gain control of our life. It is a meeting, a loving encounter with God in which we stand before him with open hands and an open heart, allowing him to touch us and transform us. Our position in prayer is not that of lowly creatures who must by force get God's attention and persuade him to listen to us. Rather, it is one in which we stir up our awareness that he is already right here where we are. We need to let his presence pervade our consciousness so that he can do his work in us.

The focus of prayer is then centered on God and not on ourselves. Prayer becomes a stance of openness in which God can do his will in us rather than we trying to bend him to our will. In this approach we cease to think of ourselves as praying, in the sense of engaging in an activity. Instead we *become* our prayer, and our whole life is gradually caught up in a prayerful attitude.

The Importance Of Listening

For this kind of growth in prayer we need to be very aware of the supreme importance of listening as a condition and a dimension of prayer. Listening is an expression of openness to another, in this instance to God, that makes it impossible to be centered on ourselves. Just as we cannot listen to another human being without forgetting ourselves, so we cannot listen to God unless we are willing to let him be the center of attention.

It is only to the degree that we become open to God that we can develop any kind of a prayerful spirit. We must always remember that it is a prayerful spirit that we strive for, not just the ability to say many prayers or even to spend long hours meditating without distraction.

God Asks Us To Listen

Listening as an aspect of prayer has many dimensions. In his revealed Scriptures, God himself repeatedly asks his people to listen to him. He all but tells them that if they do not listen to him then his whole plan for them becomes impossible.

The Book of Deuteronomy contains the basic principle of the whole Mosaic law and is used to this day as a key text in the Hebrew liturgy: "Hear, O Israel! The Lord our God is the Lord alone! Therefore you shall love the Lord our God with all your heart, with all your soul, and with all your strength" (Dt. 6:4-5). This text is best remembered from our Lord's use of it to state the first commandment of the law.

But to the Hebrews the key word in the entire text is the word "Hear," or "Listen." It was only by their listening that they would be able to make these words the norm for living that they were intended to be. A little later on in this same book God is even more emphatic in saying: "Be careful to listen to all these commandments I enjoin on you, that you and your descendants may always prosper for doing what is good and right in the sight of the Lord your God" (Dt. 12:28).

Through the prophet Isaiah, God speaks to his people: "All you who are thirsty, come to the water! . . . . Heed me and you shall eat well, you shall delight in rich fare. Come to me heedfully, listen, that you may have life" (Is. 55:1-3).

As this chapter in Isaiah continues we are given an insight into why it is so important to listen, for we are told that the ways of God are full of mystery: "For my thoughts are not your thoughts, nor are your ways my ways, says the Lord. As high as the heavens are above the earth, so high are my ways above your ways and my thoughts above your thoughts" (v. 8-9). It is clear that God is telling his people that if they really wish to enter into life with him and drink of the living waters they must be a people with listening hearts.

When we draw into the picture the person of Jesus and the riches of his kingdom, the force of these words of God take on an even greater tone of insistency for those of us who are immersed in these riches. Without a listening spirit we would be like a deaf person at a performance of Beethoven's Fifth Symphony. All the beauty and richness would be there, but it would leave the deaf person unmoved.

Listen To Jesus

When Jesus was transfigured on the mountain in the presence of his three chosen apostles, the voice from the cloud said, "This is my Son, my Chosen One. Listen to him" (Lk. 9:35). Jesus said on one occasion, "Let him who has ears to hear me, hear" (Mt. 13:9). He said to them another time, "Listen carefully to what you hear" (Mk. 4:23-24).

Perhaps the clearest insight Jesus gave us into the importance of listening is found in his parable about the farmer who went out to sow his seed (Cf. Lk. 8:2-14). We remember the basic story, how the seed fell on a variety of types of ground: the footpath, rocky soil, among briers, and finally on good and rich soil. In one of his rare explanations of a parable, Jesus explained, "The seed on good ground are those who hear the word in a spirit of openness, retain it and bear fruit through perseverance." Since the main point of the parable is the importance of hearing his word with openness, it is a powerful exhortation by Jesus that we be listening people.

There can be no doubt, then, that God himself is the first to exhort us to listen. When the message is so often repeated both in the Old Testament and in the New, it is obviously very important for us as believers.

Listening To The Revealed Word

Since God himself stresses so strongly that we listen, the obvious first source at which we are to listen to him is in his revealed word, the Scriptures. It is there, first and foremost, that we are to learn about God, ourselves and all of reality.

There are a number of ways in which listening to his word can have a powerful impact on our life of prayer. A first and very obvious application is in the hearing of his word in the daily readings of the Scriptures in the liturgy. Day by day the Church gives us an unfolding program of instruction in his word. The intention is that each day we be given some insight into the ways of God with his people. So much depends upon the attention that we bring to these daily readings.

Of course, none of us will be always perfectly attentive, and sometimes the message of the day may be so far removed from our real life that it fails to touch us in any personal way. We all have the experience of coming to the end of the readings and suddenly realizing that we do not know what has been read. Or we all know those times when a given reading fails to say much to us. Such limitations are human and to be expected.

What is important is that we cultivate the habit of listening to the readings with mind and heart, being ready and waiting should God choose to speak directly to us through them. If we do this, we will be amazed at how often a word, a saying, or an account will speak directly to us, piercing to the heart, as if it were meant only for us.

How often the reading will relate so closely to what we are experiencing at that very time. Sometimes it may not be the readings themselves but the responsorial psalm or one of the other Scriptural verses from the liturgy. This will not happen every day, but it only underlines the importance of waiting and listening for when it does happen.

Our Personal Praying Over The Scriptures

Then there is the broad area of our personal reading and praying over the Scriptures. We urgently need to nourish our spiritual lives ever more from God's revealed word. The Council Fathers of Vatican II have told us:

> In the sacred books, the Father who is in heaven meets his children with great love and speaks with them; and the force and power of God's word is so great that it remains the support and energy of the Church, the strength of faith for her sons, the food of the soul, the pure and perennial source of spiritual life" *(Constitution on Divine Revelation, #21.)*

In the same paragraph of this document, the Scriptures are placed on a parallel with the Bread of the Eucharist as a source of spiritual nourishment. Pope John XXIII coined that beautiful phrase, "the Bread and the Book," as the great sources of spiritual nourishment. In the same chapter, the Council Fathers urged that we not just read but pray the Scriptures:

> Let them remember that prayer should accompany the reading of Sacred Scriptures, so that God and man may talk together; for "we speak to him when we pray; we hear him when we read the divine saying" (Saint Ambrose) *(Ibid., #25).*

Make A Personal Collection Of Texts

Reading and praying the Scriptures, then, is an essential means of being open to God and listening to him. We all need to develop good habits of doing this. Rather than set out to read the entire Bible from cover to cover, it is better to read it selectively. From our personal reading, as well as from the texts that occur in the daily readings of the liturgy, we would do well to make our own personal collection of texts that really speak to us.

With such a collection on hand, we will never lack material for prayer. It will become a veritable gold mine of material for communing with God at those times when we can withdraw in peace and quiet to be with God.

For this type of prayer we need a listening heart. The words contain God's power within them, but they cannot affect us unless we give them entrance to our inner spirit by a listening stance. It is only by listening that God's word can become for us what the Letter to the Hebrews says it is: "Indeed, God's word is living and effective, sharper than any two-edged sword. It penetrates and divides soul and spirit, joints and marrow; it judges the thoughts and reflections of the heart" (Heb. 4:12).

This reading and praying over the Scriptures is primarily a personal help toward opening ourselves to God. But in certain instances it can take on an added dimension by reading and praying the Scriptures with others. A community may gather, or two or three friends, and in a prayerful atmosphere read and reflect together on God's word. There are many practical devices to help in this, or it can be a simple, unstructured sharing of reading, reflection, and prayer.

Listening To God In Nature

God speaks to us powerfully in his revealed Word, but this is by no means the only way he speaks to us. One of the wonderful results of listening to God's revealed Word is that it gradually gives us an all-pervading sense of his speaking to us from many sources. Certainly, one of the most important non-Scriptural ways that God speaks to us is through the things he has made, the works of nature.

Christian tradition has always been aware of this fertile source of learning about God. Jesus himself drew many of his greatest teachings from the simple things around him. He used such ordinary things as the vine, the seed, water, fire, breeze, etc., to teach his hearers the deepest truths about God and his kingdom.

For the Angelic Doctor, Saint Thomas Aquinas, it was a basic principle that we rise to the knowledge of God through the evidence of created things. There is the classic example of Saint Francis of Assisi to whom the smallest thing spoke of the glory of God and who was led to the highest mysticism through contact with the least of God's creatures.

There is a story in the life of Saint Paul of the Cross that is treasured by his sons, the Passionists. We are told that in his old age as he went for a walk in the garden he would tap the flowers with his cane and say: "Be quiet!" They spoke to him so loudly of the beauty of God. And so it has been in all of Christian tradition.

All of us need to develop a greater sensitivity to this source of hearing the voice of God. A walk through the woods, sitting by a stream or a lake, taking a flower, a leaf, or a rock into our hands and letting these things speak to us of

God can be a very fruitful source of prayer. It can gradually develop in us a sense of reverence that is at once the counterpart and the fruit of a prayerful spirit. With such a spirit we will not be absorbed by our environment but rather it will become a rich source of prayer. But once more, it is only a listening spirit that will enable us to be inspired by these many voices.

An American Indian Prayer

From the American Indian heritage we have a prayer that illustrates beautifully what we are saying here. The prayer reads:

> O great Spirit, whose voice I hear in the winds, and whose breath gives life to all the world, hear me! I need your strength and wisdom. Let me walk in beauty and make my eyes ever behold the red and purple sunset. Make my hands respect the things you have made and my ears sharp to hear your voice. Make me wise so that I may understand the things you have taught my people. Let me learn the lessons you have hidden in every leaf and rock. I seek strength, not to be greater than my brother, but to fight my greatest enemy — myself. Make me always ready to come to you with clean hands and straight eyes. So when life fades, as the fading sunset, my spirit may come to you without shame.

Listening To God In Oneself

Of all the sources at which to listen for the voice of God, the most neglected is apt to be the one closest to us — our own selves. Each of us is a vast world of unexplored mystery, each uniquely stamped by the creative finger of God and modified by a lifetime of varied experience. Hidden in the personal mystery of each of us is the face of God that awaits discovery. But most of us are in varying degrees too inexperienced, inept or simply too afraid to search very deeply into that mystery.

This area of our prayerful listening is the most difficult to speak about or analyze precisely because it is so close to us and contains so many things that we do not understand. But in spite of its difficulty, we need to work patiently at probing the mystery of our own being. Unless and until we do, there will be areas of awareness of God and of all reality that will escape us.

Until a few years ago we lived with a very neat concept of the human person as a composite of body and soul. We said that the soul had the noble faculties of intellect and will. We admitted that there were emotions but that these were to be kept in control by the higher faculties.

As for the body, we tended to think of it as a burden that held us earthbound and beyond that, the less said about it the better. That was a very easy concept to work with, and there was not much mystery in it. But all the while the mystery was really there, and it became all the more explosive by the very fact that it was ignored.

We Are More Complex

In recent years, happily, we have come to see ourselves as far more complex than our earlier concept would lead us to believe. Through the influence of the sciences of psychology, sociology and ecology, broad areas of human existence have been opened up to us. We do not deny that we are indeed made of body and soul, with intellect and will. But we see more clearly that we reach for the highest goals in a very earthbound, human condition.

The simple acknowledgment of these facts immediately opens up whole new areas of mystery and of potential discovery. It also opens up tremendous areas of listening for the voice of God as it speaks to us within the mystery of our own person and experience of life.

We hear much today about "being in touch with ourselves." The expression refers primarily to living a healthy mental and emotional life. But it also needs to be applied to what is most important in us — our life for God. This will involve a lot of exploring in fearsome territory — that inner maze of our emotions, struggles and often animal-like tendencies. It will require us to look at things we would like to turn away from as we search not just for an explanation of a human reality but for the meaning of a life that is lived in pursuit of God. It will require us to turn loose any dream we might have of ever reaching an angelic existence and convince us that the only way we will ever come to God is as human beings in a fully human arena. Any battle that is fought on a fantasy island is never the real battle. Life for God can be lived only in the real world of human existence and experience.

Discovering God's Mark In Us

Listening to our own inner self is not all darkness. It can also lead us to discover the beauty that God has placed in our own unique share of humanity. The potential that we have for good, for love, and for creativity can be discovered by us only if we are willing to look carefully and habitually at our own inner self. It is this good within that we need most of all to discover because it is the mark that God has left of himself in us and through which he speaks to us of his own infinite goodness and beauty. If we develop prayerful attitudes, it will become easier to include listening to ourselves among our habits of listening for the voice of God in our life.

Keeping A Prayer Journal

One method that many have found helpful in listening to their own person is the keeping of a spiritual or prayer journal. This is simply a matter of writing down one's inner thoughts either in the form of prayer or of reflection. In the writing itself we may not seem to be saying anything very significant. But read from hindsight we will many times discover with Jacob that "truly the Lord was in this place and I did not know it" (Gen. 28:16). We will begin to see that even in our seemingly dark moments the hand of God has been gently leading us deeper into the mystery of himself.

It may be well to state here an intuition that this writer has had for some time: that the ultimate discovery of God in this life will be made within our own inner self; that we can dream of finding in one simple gaze God, ourselves and all of reality, and they will all merge into one joyful manifestation of the greatness of God. According to this intuition, which cannot be proven, the discovery will be made through a deep meeting of God within our own person. This does not seem too impossible when we consider that all of our listening to God in his word, in nature, and in life occurs in the deep core of our being.

Listening To God In Others

Some mention should be made of the need for listening to God in our experience of one another. We are social beings and our relatedness to others forms a great part of our life. We must strive for an awareness that others are not just a source of annoyance, or a means of curbing our own selfishness, or an opportunity for practicing charity. They may be all these at times.

But even more important, each person is, as we ourselves are, a unique creation of God designed to reflect some of his own beauty and goodness. In much the same way that we need to keep our ears open to God as he speaks to us through nature and through our inner self, so we need to listen to his voice in the words and the life of others.

This can take many forms. If we notice, we will witness much good done by others through the cheerful service they render, and this can speak to us of the loving care God has for us. Through the words spoken by others we will sometimes hear and make our own insights that we might never have had ourselves.

Most important of all, there will be those few individuals in our life with whom we share our most personal experiences in our search for God. These persons become increasingly the greatest blessings on this earth because in them the goodness, love, and tender care of God are translated out of the realm of mere theory and become real flesh and blood signs of the invisible God whom we seek. Such persons give credibility to all the beautiful things God tells us about himself in his revealed Word.

Prayer And The Human Experience

Some who have read thus far may have wondered along the way: What do things like nature, the often tangled mystery of ourselves, or the people around us have to do with prayer? Some may have thought these are rather agents that we have to learn to cope with as we strive for a life of prayer.

They are indeed this, but infinitely more. They have everything to do with prayer because the only place we are ever going to grow in prayer is in the human existence that is ours. We do not and cannot come to God in a vacuum but only in the day-by-day experience of human life.

We are immersed indeed in the enfolding presence of the transcendent God who has given us his Scriptures. Even in the Scriptures he showed his face to his people and spoke to them through their day-by-day experience. It must be the same with us. We seek the transcendent God, but we come to him step by step through the hidden signs of himself that he has placed in this world in which we live.

We have a perfect example of what we have been speaking about in the person of Mary, that humble virgin of Nazareth. Hers was truly a listening heart. All her life she had listened to her God as he spoke to her in the Scriptures and in the life of her people Israel. How natural, then, that the angel should find her listening and waiting when he came to her with his message that she was chosen to be the mother of the Savior.

Through her listening Mary had come to understand that the ways of God are full of mystery. Even though she could not understand the full meaning of what the angel said to her, she could say without hesitation, "I am the maidservant of the Lord. Let it be done to me as you say" (Lk. 1:38). Her great prayer, the Magnificat, is the perfect expression of openness to God and response to him in praise of his wonderful works. She is the model, therefore, for all those who try to wait upon God with listening hearts.

8

Loneliness: Human And Christian

One of the saddest things that happens to us is our failure to bring a Christian awareness to the most ordinary human experiences. This is true in all of life but is perhaps most reflected in its painful aspects. Simple examples of this are the chronic headache, the misunderstanding of a friend or associate, or the Monday morning blahs. All of us experience these things, but for the most part they are seen as annoyances that at best are just put up with and rarely sensed as Christian experiences.

Nothing Is Untouched By Christ

If our life were merely human, perhaps this would be an appropriate reaction to the evils of life. But we are called to live a human life that is also Christian. Knowing Christ and his mystery tells us that nothing in our life is untouched by the reality of Christ. Specifically we are called to live human life as a continuation in time of the

Paschal Mystery of Christ, living out in our life that great mystery of death-resurrection that was Christ's way of redeeming us and entering so completely into our world.

Saints and spiritual writers through the ages have always spoken of the human experience as Christian experience. All that they have said is valuable and has pointed the way to holiness for people of all generations. But perhaps we perceive their message in an all too theoretical way. While appreciating the grandeur of the Christian life, we might very easily fail to see our opportunity of living it in the most ordinary things. Maybe we need fresh approaches to Christian living that focus more directly on life as we experience it in our day.

The Experience Of Loneliness

We have become a very self-analytical people, conscious of our feelings to a degree that was not possible to our forebears. The advance of psychological studies has enabled us to be consciously aware of feelings that people of former times no doubt had but did not reflect upon as we do. And all too often the discoveries we make about ourselves on the feeling level create problems that become the more acute as we are more consciously aware of them. This seems to be true especially of our experience of loneliness.

As we become more aware of ourselves and as we are given the privilege of seeing inside others through their self-revelation, we realize more and more that no human being is a stranger to loneliness. It is felt in varying degrees, of course. The deeply sensitive person seems capable of feeling it to a more intense degree, while the extrovert perhaps has more escape from its pain. But it is more and more evident that loneliness is so much a part of the human condition that not even the most intimate sharing ever completely removes it.

Loneliness is the type of experience that most people are reluctant to talk about with any degree of personal involvement. As a result, so many people, intensely aware of their loneliness, feel that they are unique. But when they get the courage to speak of their loneliness they usually find that their experience is not unique at all. They see that it is shared by enough others that it gradually dawns on them that they share this human experience in common with everyone else.

Celibate Loneliness

While all people know loneliness, the single person, the priest, and religious women and men have their own unique experience of it. The very fact of living in celibacy creates a dimension of loneliness that is different. While community life for the religious can ideally bring an experience of sharing that even marriage does not, the struggle to achieve true community can produce its own form of awareness of loneliness, just as does the struggle to attain intimacy in marriage.

The danger for the unmarried is that they begin to deal with their loneliness in an unreal way. It is easy for a single person to compare his or her lot with what is imagined to be the fulfillment of total sharing in marriage. Such a person can come to think that his or her loneliness is a direct result of the celibate state and that it would automatically be remedied if this person were married.

What this one does not think of is that there are many married people who, in frustration, dream of the single or religious state as an ideal situation for the solution of all human problems including that of loneliness. Perhaps what is needed is more dialogue between Christian married people and celibates. Such dialogue could make both married persons and celibates more realistically aware that the problem is not in their way of life but in the human condition which they share in common.

Beware Of Too Simple An Answer

From the outset we must beware of giving too simplistic an interpretation of and solution to the problem of loneliness. Some may be tempted to make a statement something like this: we need to sublimate our loneliness and find a remedy for it in the intimacy of Christ's love.

This is a true statement of principle, but it assumes too much to be of help to one who feels deeply the pain of loneliness. It implies that we can sublimate by a mere act of our will, and it is not that easy. It further assumes that we really grasp the depth and personal nature of Christ's love for us. As a matter of fact, most of us come to a personal grasp of the love of Jesus only very slowly and gradually. So it is simply not enough to invoke a spiritual principle and expect an easy solution.

Inserting The Spiritual Principle

It needs to be stressed that we can never solve a human problem by merely applying a spiritual principle. This is not to say that the spiritual principle is not vitally necessary to the solution. It only means that the spiritual principle can be effective only when it is inserted fully into the real human situation and when the human problems have been understood, accepted and worked through on their own level. I suspect that most of us have wasted a lot of time and energy and endured a lot of frustration through failing to understand this in a practical way.

We must, first of all, be willing to face the fact of our loneliness squarely and not try to deny its existence. We must be willing to feel the pain of loneliness and accept it as part of the human condition. Any stance that fails to do this opens the door to all sorts of sham battles with oneself and with others, even God.

Then we must be willing to recognize for what they are the many forms of escape we tend to take from our loneliness. Since we find loneliness painful we instinctively and subconsciously look for relief. This escape can take many forms: indulging in endless distraction, overtly seeking the acceptance of others, seeking fulfillment in being useful rather than in becoming, the use of anesthetics such as alcohol, drugs, tobacco and many others. All of these things could have other causes, of course. But if we are seeking to make peace with our own loneliness, we need at least to examine such tendencies to see if through them we might just be seeking escape from loneliness.

A Means Of Growth

Far more important, however, is the effort to convert our experience of loneliness into an instrument of growth. Much of our loneliness comes from failure to discover the goodness that is within us. Early experiences and training so often have a way of leaving us with a very negative self-image. It does us no good to waste time and energy bemoaning this fact. Rather, the awareness of it should be a signal to begin from where we are and try to enter upon the path of discovery of our own goodness and riches. To deny that goodness is there is to deny the goodness of our Creator who sees that all his works are good.

At this point we might ask the question: why does God create us as limited beings? Pursuit of this question would lead us deep into the realm of God's mysterious designs. But it seems that we approximate an answer when we say that he wanted us to discover through our limitations the grandeur of dependence upon him. In this very discovery it seems that God has a way of revealing to the humble soul the beauty within itself that could not be discovered until God himself was found.

An Experience Of Death

In a very real sense, the pain of loneliness is an experience of death. It is a form of pain that touches all of us deeply, and no amount of wishing will take it away. We could see this pain as just one of the inevitable annoyances of life on earth and endure it in a stoical way. But as Christians we are called to more than that. We are invited to see loneliness as a part of our share in the cross of Christ that casts its shadow over all of life and through it to let ourselves feel something of the pain of Christ in his passion.

But even when we do this we have not yet made peace with the mystery of loneliness. The mystery of Christ and of redemption did not end with his death. Through death he entered into life — the glorious life of resurrection.

When Jesus calls us to share his cross in any way he always includes the invitation to pass through death to life. In this instance he calls us through the death of loneliness to know the life of inner solitude. It is there that God is found and with him the mystery of our own being and of all reality.

The Mystery Of Inner Solitude

The mystery of inner solitude is the sunny side of the mystery of loneliness. It is like the inside of a stained glass window, where the nondescript outer appearance becomes all light and color. Without our ability to feel loneliness there would be no ability to discover the life of inner solitude.

We are pained by loneliness when we focus on the fact that we are so distinct and individual that we can never merge completely with another, even God. We discover inner solitude when we accept and rejoice in the fact that only in our distinct inner self can we really find God. Finding him there we can go out in love and service to others and in turn find God anew in them. Loneliness is the unredeemed experience of our individuality. Solitude is the experience of the same reality when we finally come to know ourselves as redeemed and loved by God.

Words elude us as we try to analyze this mystery that is so deeply embedded in human life. But enough light is present to at least glimpse the truth that in this mystery so close to us is hidden the key to the discovery of God, ourselves, and all reality.

Jesus said it all when he said, "If anyone wants to be a follower of mine, let him renounce himself and take up his cross and follow me. For anyone who wants to save his life will lose it; but anyone who loses his life for my sake will find it" (Mt. 16:24-25).